qarrtsiluni

online literary magazine

Qarrtsiluni is an experiment in online literary and artistic collaboration. The title comes from an Iñupiaq word that means "sitting together in the darkness, waiting for something to burst."

The online journal began publishing on September 20, 2005; our first print issue was the September-December issue, 2008.

We encourage you to visit our website, where in addition to all the material presented here, you will find audio files of the authors reading their own work, music and video contributions to the theme, full-color reproductions of all the images, comments from readers and responses from the authors.

www.qarrtsiluni.com

Dave Bonta

managing editor

Beth Adams

managing editor and designer

ISBN 978-0-9781749-5-8

Printed in the United States

PHOENICIA PUBLISHING
MONTREAL

mutating the signature

january–april 2009

Let's get two things straight: Collaboration isn't incarceration or incorporation.

True, collaboration is like incarceration in that handcuffs, particularly the kind lined with faux fur, are absolutely necessary. The collaborative process works best when participants are attached but still able to reach with their free hands. Of course, by "free," we mean within the context of their material conditions (e.g. diet, geography and astrological determiners).

Collaboration is also like a company in that profit is collected. However, paychecks come in the form of beads and trinkets. Threading these requires a keen eye and a bottle of aspirin. Sharing a set of contact lenses is not advisable, since blurred vision leads to the most desirable outcomes. This is art, after all, not a driving test. Nobody wants or needs collaborative art taking up valuable space on our already congested highways.

Like a brain in the gut, collaborative process challenges the ego. Thoughts smear like cheap mascara on an overly emotional drag queen, which is not to say the collaborative process is overly emotional. In focus groups, collaboration has been called "impersonal" and "emotionally unavailable." That's right: Collaboration is your father. However, collaboration has also scored high in the areas of "inappropriate staring" and "monkey business."

We applaud those who undertook collaboration for this issue. We sympathize with your resulting identity crises and ecstatic spasms. Unfortunately, we only have poetic licenses, which means we can't dole out any medications to help you return to your isolation chambers. Soon the word "I" will disappear from your vocabulary. You won't notice when it goes, but might later feel mild tingling and foreign-body sensations in your ribs.

There will also be a slight awkwardness when ordering at restaurants. People will wonder why you always order for two. They will assume you are using the royal "we." They will never understand you. You are an artist. You are not meant to be understood. Thank you.

Dana Guthrie Martin and Nathan Moore
editors

Contents

Let's Mess it Up Again

The King Canutes

Cover art by Peregrine Honig (watercolor) and Drew Padrutt (design)

It was cold for spring I pulled my coat around me as I walked you to your car
whistling a kiss is just a kiss, well, is that just what they are?
I would kiss you if I thought you thought that I could stand the strain
Do you really want another chance to mess things up again?

I was sleeping when you said hello, I thought it was a dream
about a ghost that I used to know back from the foreign war
Said you'd come to make it up to me, would I make it up to you?
You can smile all you want but it won't count for yesterday no, no
    It's all right, I'm the same,
    it's all right, just the good remains,
    I cried away the shame

Maybe days spent apart have done us good though I never thought they would
but the strings it took me years to untangle now I pull around me like a long lost favorite shirt
I remember staying up all night when your perfume made me drunk
Now, whose idea was it to leave,
    I don't recall (it's all right)
    and I don't mind, it's all right,
    yeah it's only time, it's all right
    Have we always known
    that this time would come and go?

It was cold for spring I pulled my coat around me as I walked you to your car
Whistling a kiss is just a kiss, well, is that just what they are?
And I never will forget it, it's like a picture, your face lit up in the neighbor's headlights
he just sat there as you held me and we leaned against your car
I would kiss you if I thought you thought that I could stand the strain
Do you really want another chance

    Let's mess it up again, let's mess it up again

and even if the finer things are behind us now,
the brighter days, you know
That it's all right, I don't mind,
let's mess it up again, it's all right

The King Canutes are: Richard Alwyn Fisher (vocals, acoustic and baritone guitars, writer) and Keir Woods (omnichord, backing vocals), with a shifting cast of other musicians. On this track: Scott Johnson (drums, percussion and slide guitar), Seryn Potter (vocals), Dana Kletter (vocals), Alex Cox (bass), Margaret White (violins), Anna Callner (cello), Jim Bentley (recording and mixing), and Scott Easterday (string arrangement).

Listen to the .mp3 at http://qarrtsiluni.com/2009/01/15/lets-mess-it-up-again/

Process notes

Richard and Keir had recorded the entire album in 2006, but their digital masters were stolen just before Keir left the States. They have spent the past two years re-creating Last Callers and Losers, with Richard in New York and Keir in Paris. Richard writes:

> *There were collaborations between Keir Woods and me initially on the arrangements. Scott Easterday did the string arrangements. The cover was a collaboration between Peregrine Honig and the designer Drew Padrutt, after Peregrine and I went back and forth on what it was going to be a picture of. Jim Bentley and I sent versions of mixes back and forth to Keir in Paris trying to get it sorted out to where we were all happy. It's crazy collaboration all over this record.*

We also can't resist, in this time of interregnum in the U.S., quoting from the album description at CD Baby:

> *The band takes its name from King Canute, ancient king of England, legendary for failing to halt the onrushing tide. Two apocryphal stories exist for his motivations: One claims his arrogance propelled him to have his throne set up in the surf, where the unyielding waves famously swept him away. Others suggest his true motivation lay in proving to a sycophantic court the limit of a king's power.*

Alwyn and Woods trade in such dichotomies and ambiguities within their songs, where characters struggle with the ramifications of their decisions.

Evolution of the Signature

Emily May Anderson and Samantha Meyers

When I was young I used to sit and write my name over and over.
More often I would trace the names of enemies and their histories.
Their names always seemed much more interesting, more beautiful,
than mine and with only twenty-six letters to play with I forgave them
their fallacies, that my letters were dull, lacking in exotica, that this reflected
something about myself. It was so simple, the act of writing, yet
the repercussions linger. I have scrawled this name thousands of times,
on checks, birthday cards, love letters, and it has taken years for my name
to become my identity, each letter irrevocably mine but also part of something
larger, unnamed, unwieldy, like a forged and forgotten sword
that cuts to the truth: history is composed of letters like mine.

History is proud and permanent, unable to transcend itself
and become more than words on a page. History is the high school jock
who concerns himself only with practical jokes and petite blondes
all his life, and one day finds himself forty years old, still
living in his parents' basement, no relationship lasting longer
than a six pack or a football game, his purpose lost in the past.

History is like that: devolved from a true story into memory,
sagging and tired, but history allows astute lovers to search out
the foreign. Fingers trace a different alphabet, Cyrillic or Arabic or
Greek, an exchange between two lovers who communicate only by touch;
fingers say the unsayable, run across skin, support the arch
of the spine, dance over the flat perfection between breasts, and the gentle slope
of stomach. I can touch every desire and its corresponding part. Hold me
closer than you think you should. Let me in to the lowest register,
dip your pen below the blue line, deep enough that we know this is real,
but not painful to the point of childhood. I used to sit alone
and write my name, my future unmet but anticipated. If I would have known
that all things come to this, I would not have wasted so much time
tracing patterns that mean nothing. I will keep you and hide letters in pockets.

Process notes

Emily writes: Sam and I wrote this poem line-by-line, in American Sentences. It was an interesting experience because we both came in to the project with our own ideas, and writing one line at a time forced each of us to work with the other's ideas as well as our own. It was frustrating at times because when I would hand her the notebook, I would have no idea where her line would take the poem. By the end, we had worked in ideas from both of us. I did a first revision, and chose not to keep the poem in seventeen syllable lines. She supported that decision, and we then did a second revision together, and realized we both liked where the poem had gone.

dance

Andrew Topel and Paul Brandt

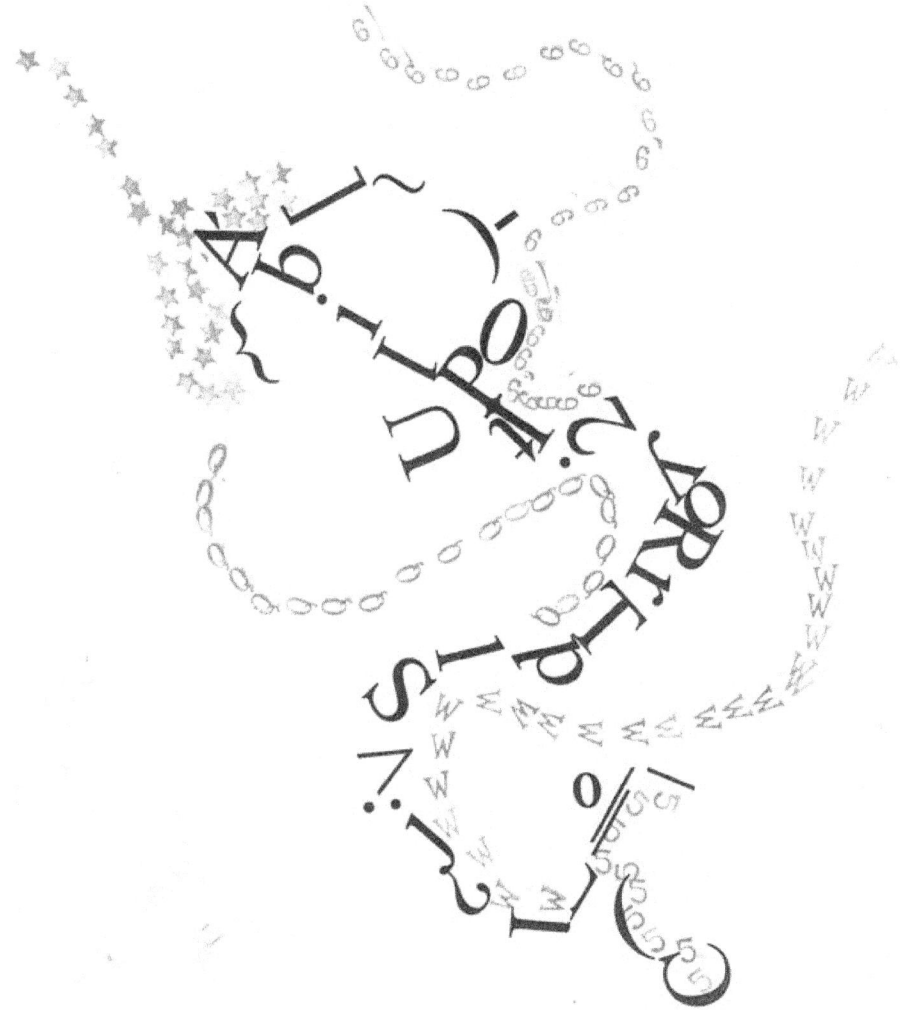

Process notes

Paul writes: All I can really say about this collaboration is that I was trying to do my part in this extension of our friendship.

Oracle at Acres of Books

Greta Aart and Sally Molini

A capella in the Greek and Roman
                stacks, the woman clears
        her throat. She seems to like
moderato cantabile, sings on her knees,
                a babble of feeling
out of her life into mine.

Hair wild, body masking
                new paperback smell, soon
        she'll be asked to leave
the slick unbroken
                spines that keep in tact
days of the market god, a pillar

with the bearded head of Hermes.
                Back then, you laid
        a coin on the altar before whispering
                a question in his ear.
The answer: first words heard outside.

Her voice is good, a chanson in some painful
                minor key. Notes falter, the manager arrives.
        I slip away, pay for my books. Tom
                behind the counter hands
me a receipt, wishes me good night –

his eyes never meet mine, as if we shared
                some guilty past. Two smokers laugh
        outside the door, kicking up snow.
                We're not helpless!
yells one of them. Stamping their feet,
they go back inside, tired of being cold.

Vanishing Biography

Buddha smiles because nothing is
static, so why label and hammer
a story on someone's grave?
There's always that backdrop
of the next frame
even when it's empty,
even when filled with Edith Piaf
singing, whose heart stoked every note,
whose voice knew nothing could stop
the locomotive bend of a willow.
Conditions move on —
that's why mountains don't grow on clouds
like the human mind does, projecting
motives onto the wind, wanting to know
whether it prefers east or west.

Process notes

Collaboration in any form of artistic endeavour is not exactly about working together. It is more about trust — trusting each partner's instincts. The phrase "working together," so often overused, implies a measured and controlled working process. In reality, any collaboration must always fall short of such idealistic harmony before it is truly a collaborative effort. Once an effort involves more than one person, unknown factors arise, and should arise. We like to think that what makes collaboration intriguing is this element of seemingly open-ended obscurity, an inability to know exactly what the other artist or writer is thinking. Precisely because of such uncertainty, an intuitive trust can grow even stronger.

Writing poetry, like any form of writing, is quinessentially a solitary activity. When we collaborated in making a poem, the entire process was a combination of two solitudes. Each of us first began the creation of two unfinished poems; sometimes it was just jotting down some lines or a stanza or two, with the deliberate intention of leaving ample room for the other party's creativity. Both of us needed to be sensitive towards each other's line aesthetics, poetic "breath," imagist modes, as well as preferred word choice and colors. Collabora-

tion was obviously in the back of each of our minds from the start, yet we were in our own solitudes, so there also existed a space that belonged to Sally and to Greta. On "Vanishing Biography," for instance, Greta wrote it as a compilation of five koan-like verses, each finished and complete. At the same time, she tried to have every image or line open to new narrative or lyrical voices, wrote without thinking of "controlling" each verse, and to a certain degree, did not worry about a fixed context. As we each wrote our two poems, we both realised that there was not much point in wondering how the other would respond to them, unless each of us wanted to control her response, which, of course, was not the point of our collaboration. As it turned out, Sally wove in new, accompanying images or circumstance, so that an additional layer of narrative could thread through the collage. Theme still remains, but there was now a new story, and a different energy. This surprise was exhilarating.

Greta lives in Paris, France, and Sally lives in Omaha, Nebraska, so they corresponded by email. There was some "hazing" of our "signatures" in terms of polishing, cutting, altering and re-writing, but a crucial part of the process, and what made it so meaningful, was realizing the unexpected range and creativity of two imaginations instead of one.

From a 2005 (and on-going) collaboration of poem-sculptures and text-poems

Nick Carbó and Eileen R. Tabios

The collaboration between Nick Carbó and Eileen R. Tabios unfolded through snailmail, with each sending a sculpture that generates a poem:

1) Nick sends a sculpture comprised of a toilet regulator painted with the following words:

Can you regulate
The flow of desire

2) Eileen responds by sending a wooden box recycled from once containing wine bottles of Screaming Eagle. The phrase "Screaming Eagle" is emblazoned, along with the image of an eagle in flight, against the box. The box contains long ribbons designed to spill forth when the box is opened. Attached to the side of a box is a toilet's flusher mechanism. The accompanying poem:

Trap the intangible
to release

Desire most beautiful
when unleashed

3) Nick replies by sending a blue box containing Alka Selzer tablets upon which are incribed letters. When the box is opened, the tablets spell out the following poem:

Take one Saussarian pill 3X daily to induce / Desire

This is how the cerulean curve
of her spine presents pink
ideas at four in the afternoon

where words become
arbitrary trees, cones
intangible blues

This is how the
release feels at the tip
of the tongue when pressed

against his wet
red frenulum slippery
with meaning

4) Eileen responds by sending four stacking boxes, correlated to four stanzas of a poem. Each stanza written on the inside cover of a box. Boxes are colored blue and white. Stacked atop each other with a white ribbon tying them together. All must be unwrapped in order to go through sculpture. Eileen very much wanted to include (the bodies of) the audience (reader/viewer) into the sculpture by having their involvement through the process of unwrapping the boxes.

The first box contains a pearl necklace cellophane-wrapped in its middle so that it's not possible to wear it. The second box contains an American Red Cross pin referencing breast cancer. The third box contains used ribbons from unwrapped gifts. The fourth box contains a grey sports bra overlaid with a pretty lacey bra.

Inside the fourth box, the stanza is encompassed within a circle, as formed by a "Filipino poet" symbol's belly (from an earlier project by Eileen Tabios entitled "Poems Form/From The Six Directions"). The bras are "convex with concave." The accompanying poem:

Untitled

Surely we
Never wish
To stray

From bodies

Those curves
Offering possibilities

For
"the convex with the concave"

Dear Seven: A Circle of Epistles
Part 1 in a series of 7

cin salach

Dear Mike,

a man walks into a bar and finds a good view.

How are you?

his words rest heavy on the table.

I feel self-conscious as if I'm thinking this under a bright light.

he wonders how the light found parking on such a dark night.

Right now it's pouring rain, really pouring, rolling thunder and crashes of lightning which feels out of place for November. I just got back from an appointment with my acupuncturist. While I was on the table I thought about this poem. How awkward it felt until joy broke through and I realized I could use your help lifting heavy things. A man! Between you and me, lately I have been tiring of being a strong woman. Strong like a man and strong like a woman. Chopping wood. Carrying water. Shopping for candles. Working to feed the babies and the wife. She's starting her own business you know.

he's been saying this for years.

Thunder and lightning are shaking the house at this moment. The animals are jumpy but I am sitting in the window writing this and enjoying myself very much. Have you ever noticed I have large hands? I prefer to keep them empty but it's been a struggle these past few months. I want to fill them with air I have brought back from our land in Wisconsin. Did I tell you I am a landowner? Maybe that's why I crave mud. The color. The smell. The weight. My acupuncturist said it's understandable why some women want to eat dirt and I wish I had a big plate of it because I can taste the rich earth and I can feel my bones getting stronger. I can feel everything about me lengthening into the ground.

What do men crave?

Sincerely,

cin

Part 2

Mike Puican

Dear Alice

Different things were happening at the same time. The street thrashed like a low grade fever, hail leapt from the grass! There you were at that dim grocery store of the dying mill town. The eight-months pregnant checkout girl was watching CNN as you wandered Produce grasping for Ariadne's thread. Your only guides: oblivion and the possible lack of nerve.

I watched as your heart turned into Frozen Desserts and you held the toy steering wheel pretending to steer the cart. Tonight as you sit at your desk in a mildewed basement, asbestos sifting from the floorboards, the black waters of Lethe smoking past the ash tree in the back yard, you lean toward its calm.

Part 3

Alice George

Dear Mary —

I would like to talk about rooms. William Gass proposed that a book is a building for what the brain has spun. So a letter is a room. Your husband's letter to me was full of location, as if he and therefore I were rapidly beaming in and out of chaos: Captain Kirk and his obedient lackey. Basements and parking lots, orchestra pits and grocery stores. He is so active, your guy. (But when we sit at the table, he is stalwart at your side.) I want this letter to be a little sendable bag for what my sleepy Sunday brain is knitting. Wooden needles click.

I am writing to you from a new room. An old room in our 120 year-old house, the room that was first my son's then my daughter's and now refitted for the son again in preparation for his return from college. Everything is IKEA neat right now, the only muss the dust on top of the plastic fortune-telling Buddha, the one I gave him last Christmas, the one sitting on some glib western manufacturer's idea of buddha responses, like *look within.*

Content as a mug of tea here, because Sam will return in a few days. We hung a long green batiked scarf in the window and everything is now watery green, my hands as I write you, my pajamas, his posters and books. A moist, dim green against the November outside.

If letters are little knitted compartments of saying, then I should hurry and say before I run out of yarn. Your daughter is a temple. My daughter is a swimming pool. Your daughter is an atrium. We are both splendid galleries within the museum of this city. You are a library stacked with real wisdom, truly. Your daughter is a volleyball court. My son is somewhere in Boston now, his body a concert hall, his eyes will be blue all the way back to Chicago.

Yours, Alice

PS Don't show this to Mike yet, he needs to wait.

Part 4

Mary Hawley

Dear Cecilia,

I would have written sooner but this week I was sick with not a bad cold but a good one, the kind that leaves you so tired and dizzy you want only to sleep, and sleeping is justified. So while Mike wrote and fixed things and went to the Y I drifted through dreams: my brother, a child again, waving a jeweled bug full of precious, poisonous serum; a room of watery green; an art gallery where a toddler clung to George Bush's legs and said Grandpa, Grandpa. Now I am better.

Since we don't know each other well it might be good to ask questions:

- Do you like Japanese movies?
- Under what circumstances would you fire a gun?
- What has more poetry in it: a fire or a swing?

One day of my childhood I sat on a swing with a wide wooden seat. I was alone, it was sunny, two stout ropes disappeared into the leaves above me. The swing creaked under me. The air tasted of morning. I have looked for that swing ever since.

Cecilia is my mother's name and I always wished it were mine, musical name like the three-note song of a bird, name of the patron saint of music. My mother had a small marble carving of St. Cecilia lying dead, a gash in her neck to show how they couldn't behead her (at first). While Mary the Mother of God was, after all, only a mother, meaning laundry and dishes, the odd night out at a wedding. When I spent my Communion money to baptize a pagan baby in China, I named her Cecilia.

Yesterday I put away all my garden pots, first soaking them in water. The pots come from the Dominican Republic, China, Italy, USA — their origins stamped into the clay. But no sign of the hands that slopped the clay into molds, carried them to the kilns for firing. I soak the pots because clay dries out over time, and then the soil in the pots dries out too quickly. When you plunge a dry clay pot into water it sings for a long time, hissing tea-kettle notes as water finds its way back into the spaces. In the spring I will fill them again with dirt and then marigolds, geraniums, lobelia, coleus.

One of the nuns next door is Italian, so they chat in Italian while unloading the groceries or grilling on their tiny back porch. They do not know much about St. Cecilia, but they are dedicated to St. Francis, patron saint of animals and the environment. Yesterday they poured us shots of sambuca for a Thanksgiving toast. Sambuca has the sting of black licorice, is made with star anise and elder flowers. My fingers, coiled around the glass, were stained with dirt. The drink lit a sweet fire in my throat before I went back to soaking the pots.

May words be a sweet fire in your throat, Cecilia.

Mary

Part 5

Cecilia Pinto

Chris,

I hope this letter finds you well.

Here is what I think I want to tell you.

I sleep on my left side with one leg out, one leg curled in, and one arm out and the other curled in. I read once that this is an indication of an essential conflict of self.

Possums live in our garage. Our dog will carry one around in her mouth while the possum plays dead. Even though the animal appears lifeless, its heart is beating. When we tell the dog to drop it, the possum scuttles away to hide amid gardening tools, clay pots, bags of mulch and dirt.

My husband built a boat which hangs in the rafters of the garage. You can row it or sail it. He thought, after his mother died, that his father would like a wood-working project to distract him from his grief. So he bought the plans for the boat and set the project up in his father's garage. But his father never took an interest and so Jim built the boat in our garage. His father died a year and a half after his mother.

We've used the boat once; me, Jim and our boys, Henry and Grant. We floated.

Sometimes as we drift off to sleep, my husband will apologize for his tiredness saying, *I'm sorry, my train is leaving the station.* And then we depart each other, even as we sleep together.

Babies and small children often sleep on their backs, arms flung out, because they are not conflicted and worry about nothing.

Yesterday in the woods, our dog found a huge, dead bird. It lay, split wide open, black feathers and red guts. The dog did not touch the bird.

My father says that my Italian grandfather courted my Irish grandmother by taking her rowing. I picture my grandmother's pale, soft beauty, my grandfather's sweat and desire. My father would never use the word desire to tell this story.

I am trying to decide if the fact that I don't know you is making this easier or harder to write?

Once, when we were visiting my husband's parents, they offered to take our first child, Henry, so we could sleep in. I saw them, smiling down at our sleepy, milky baby, nestled between them in their own bed.

Sometimes, when our boys were sleeping babies, I'd want to wake them, to make sure they were alive, and because I missed them so much.

Lately, we've been killing mice. The traps are not always effective. Two nights ago, Henry, who is almost twenty now, found a mouse with one tiny paw stuck in the trap. He flailed violently until Henry released him, then he ran away. All of this bothered Henry, as it would anyone, I think.

I went to bed late last night but Henry wasn't home yet. My first thought this morning was, *where is Henry?* I looked in his room. He was asleep on his back, one arm crossed over his head, partially covering his face.

The mice run through our house, I've met them on the stairs.

As I write this, my husband is awake, our sons still asleep. They drift, they float. If I wake them, they will stare at me speechless, momentarily without words or memory.

I have a book on my shelf called, *Winter Sleeping Animals*. I bought it because I thought the title was so beautiful. It's a children's book that describes the ways and reasons that animals hibernate. I recall another children's book I used to read to the boys about a family of bears that awoke from hibernation to celebrate Valentine's Day.

Chris, I hope you sleep like a baby and that every morning begins with wordlessness and love.

Cecilia

Part 6

Chris Green

Dear cin,

I'm writing to say hello. We are new friends. Which means I know you and I don't. So, I will be the protagonist of this letter, you will be the ghost.

New friend, you "have land" in Wisconsin! I promise to teach you how to fly fish. I'll tell you this: casting is a beautiful dance, and there's nothing as luxurious as standing in a stream, but you need to accept that fish are not abstract. Catching a fish is like looking into the face of every mistake you've ever made — the eyes, innocent golden disks, look and look. And yet to cradle the fish in its slick gasping skin, free the hook and slip the body back into velvet… Life must be lived to be understood.

An odd moment: a squirrel fat as a small raccoon is scratching at my screen. He refuses to face the music. Winter is dawning on us. Ice weights the trees, each branch like white coral. My roof, who knows the ordinary boringness of a house, is silent while snow humps up in the road.

Recently, I found a list of goals in an old notebook:

1. Learn the mandolin
2.
3.

I keep my invisible mandolin under wraps — the future gleams, and my dread of 2 and 3.

I think of this thing about happiness, and our promise to emptiness. Each morning I wake, say I'm sorry out loud, to myself. In emergencies, I quote my favorite poetry — a poem Lexa wrote at eleven years old:

No it isn't   no it's not
Yes it is   it's getting quite hot.
Summer is out   Summer is in.
Summer is here   so let's go swim.

I once heard you read at the Green Mill, something about the inevitability of men and road construction in spring. Actually, you don't read, you sing. Teach me! I'll wait for you with my loving mandolin — we'll sing something something something about my mother's mismarriage and its residue.

I once asked you if it was true, "Girls levitate each other at slumber parties?" You rose to a witchy laugh and looked at me. You said it's easy — mothers, girlfriends, wives and daughters all know. Why aren't scientists studying this and winning awards? No magic but science is how I see things, yet with two fingers you've raised whole girls in pajamas and white socks… light as a feather stiff as a board. Boys don't float, we play tackle basketball and swear and weigh ourselves down in forts.

cin, I should have written more about children. We will both be living the truth of babies soon. I don't know what to say. From here, below zero, I can only quote William Matthews, "Our children are the only message we can leave them."

Keep well,

Chris

P.S.

Editor's note: This letter was published in Columbia Poetry Review no. 20, 2007, and is reprinted here to preserve the integrity of the series.

Part 7

Eileen Favorite

Dear Chris,

It's been two years since the letter went 'round and I've been two years waiting for the break in the day. Not the daybreak, for like any new mother/father I've seen plenty of those, what Sylvia Plath called Nicholas' "bald cry" which took "its place among the elements." You've had it times two with your twin girls, and what a flickering whirlwind of a carousel ride it is, it is. Baby girls all around.

I hope our girls get together someday and levitate. I did it too, just like cin. You were only supposed to lift with two fingers, but somebody always cheated. Did you know that before the levitation happened, there was a séance? One girl would sit with the floatee's head in her lap. She'd rub the floatee's temples and tell everyone gathered around the story of how she died. "One night, Marguerite was walking along the road beside the graveyard. Dot dot dot." Closing your eyes and listening to the story of your death felt holy and silly; you were spooked and yet delighted to still be alive! The final verse was *light as a feather stiff as a board, let's raise Marguerite up to the Lord.*

When my cousins came over we played "Mary Widoworth." Holding a candle, we faced the bathroom mirror in the dark, chanting, "I believe in Mary Widoworth, I believe in Mary Widoworth. Mary Widoworth, if you're there, give us a sign!" Then one of my older siblings would pound on the wall (the other bathroom lined up behind it), and we'd all go screaming into the hall. Mary Widoworth was much hokier than levitation, but standing in the dark looking into a mirror with a flickering candle and then screaming your head off and bursting into the light was so magnificent, we easily suspended our disbelief.

I wonder if you believe in psychics, Chris. I have no psychic abilities, myself, but I'm convinced that others do. Would you think that silly?

And there it is, the ring of the phone, then the waking cry of Lulu, which drags me away from this epistle. Her cry is no longer a bald fright, but a whiny demand. She loves words, as we all do; she'll repeat whatever you say — not always clearly, and not always correctly, but she rejoices in language and that makes me glad.

In honor of all sleepovers and cousins, I sign this with the grade school salutation:
sorry so short stupid and sloppy

Ciao,
Eileen

The authors are, in order: cin salach, Mike Puican, Alice George, Mary Hawley, Cecilia Pinto, Chris Green, and Eileen Favorite. They write:

We — the seven poets whose work will appear here under the title of "Dear Seven: A Circle of Epistles" — have been meeting regularly for two years to challenge ourselves in the writing of forms and various other poetic adventures. Each month a new form or project is proposed; the following month we share our efforts. The resulting work offers us a chance to compare and contrast how we each approach each month's "assignment." The creation of "Dear Seven" was a defining moment for the group as we adapted the collaborative surrealist concept of "Exquisite Corpse" to the epistolary form. Over a month, a chain of letters was created, in which each poet only saw the letter they received, and the one they created in response. Then we assembled and read them in order, enjoying the surprising echoes and themes which emerged.

Giver of Givens

K. Alma Peterson and Kathleen Jesme

No longer am I drawn to speak in simple diagrams
as my father's notebooks travel with me to the endpoints
of a tangle he labeled every operation and eased
with friendly question every knot pretty much
in line with the finish which appears to travel westward
to the wilds of theory where phrases like rotations are simply turns
last modified momentarily by brilliant sun on new snow:
he said years of flying in the far north
gave him a touch of snowblindness
and something else he kept back
as he traveled westward in his small plane
through the wilds and toward evening.

Process notes

We decided to try this collaboration because we are both sound-oriented poets, and we wanted
to try a dialog in which we listened to each other and let the sound lead us. We each started a
thread, and responded to each other's additions on a daily basis, each adding a new thread each day.
Eventually, we were responding to six threads every day. We kept this going for two weeks. It was a
madhouse! There was no time to evaluate what we were writing — the idea was to push ourselves to
produce a large body of material. Then we got together and read everything, and picked out threads
and sequences we liked. We did more work on them, mostly editing, and arrived at the three collaborative poetic dialogs that we are submitting to Qarrtsiluni.

Found Photo

Peter Cherches and Holly Anderson

When you live with something long enough I guess you get used to the odor and then it's no odor at all, it's part of the room, maybe it's just a dead mouse behind the wall and there's nothing to be done unless you want to take a hammer to the wall one hot, grey afternoon when it feels like ants are crawling up and down your legs, getting right into your underpants.

So here we are, all dressed up and left all alone in the shaking woods. Why did they leave us out here like this, all alone? Drive away in that brand new automobile we helped them to buy? Sure, Pop's lost a bit of his left leg, the diabetes chewed his foot right up to the shinbone, but that's no reason to throw us out here without so much as a drink of water. A smell, sure, but not a stink. And weren't they the ones always pushing sugary things at him anyway? He never was one to say no.

When you live with something long enough it's really no odor at all.

We knew it had to come off when even the dogs wouldn't go near him.

Thinking helps to pass the time.

He never did talk much, and it's especially hard to be sitting here on a bench in the absolute dead center of nowhere with a one and a half-legged man who won't say a word. Thank the Lord they didn't drive off with the crutches.

When you live with something long enough I guess you get used to it.

So here we are, left alone in the woods by our own children, and not a soul to help us, and not a drop to drink. My mouth must look like a flattened mattress by now. Or an old and faded photograph.

It's all part of life, I guess. You bring them into this world, you do your best to make a life for them, and then they have to up and leave you one day, go off on their own. I just never thought it would be like this! It's like there's dead mouse behind the wall and there's nothing to be done unless you want to take a hammer to the wall one hot, grey afternoon when it feels like ants are crawling up and down your legs, getting right into your underpants, out in the woods, all alone, thinking to pass the time, sitting on a bench with a one and a half-legged man who won't say a word.

An old and faded photograph has an odor, but not a stench.

They had collaborated once before, about eighteen years earlier, but the piece they wrote then was published for the first time only recently. That publication led to an invitation to submit to the present collection. They agreed that it would be nice to work together again, and they started tossing ideas back and forth via email. Time constraints wouldn't allow the two of them to get together in a room and compose a piece from scratch through give and take, as they had done before. They'd have to work differently this time. One of them suggested that they each write independent sections of a prose piece, or intertwined sentences, with different typefaces to differentiate the two voices (though they would not identify which typeface matched which contributor). The other wasn't happy with that idea, didn't want the individual contributions to be so clearly delineated. This one suggested a process whereby each would submit a piece to the other, a piece the first writer felt was unfinished, perhaps, or just not up to snuff, and the second would work with it: edit it, change it, complete it, rewrite it, whatever seemed appropriate, whatever seemed in order. The version completed by the second writer would be the final version. The writer who started the piece would have no veto power and no rights to further edit or rework it. The writer who suggested this method saw this as an exercise in trust. Two writers with different but compatible voices and visions would have their way with each other's pieces. They would not reveal which of them started which piece. The other writer was skeptical at first, felt that their individual voices would be flattened or neutralized by the process. But the writer who suggested this method didn't see it that way at all. This writer believed that the process could unleash a compelling third (or third and fourth) voice, a product of the two. The other ultimately agreed to this approach. The two writers submitted old, long-abandoned (or shunted aside) pieces to each other, and they went to work. Two pieces, by two writers.

Winding

Jo Hemmant, Michelle McGrane and Christine Swint

The river gave no sign
of where she might have drifted.
It carried the sky and trees like roots.

Leaves traced hieroglyphics
along the snaking spine of a gravel path
that led to the road. Cars passed

in transit, unwilling to stop
for a vine-draped shadow glimpsed
at the edge of light.

Arney's girl was seen
near the rubble at the old quarry,
pale limbs twined with weeds,

curls of ivy on crumbling stone.
A fusion of need and air,
we reached for her like

drowning victims emerging
wild to claw the sun.
When the search parties stopped,

the land was changed.
We returned to the river,
its flux her blood.

Process notes

We started with a raw video of clips Christine shot while running errands in her town. After Michelle and Jo viewed the video, Michelle suggested a theme of 'disappearance,' and came up with a rough outline for a narrative that we all liked. There were a few images and scenes that Jo felt didn't quite go with our intended poem, which we later deleted. We didn't know how the lines would turn out, but we did have an idea of where we were going from the start.

Writing line by line, we alternated between the three of us via Facebook, a convenient option since Jo lives in England, Michelle is in South Africa, and Christine is in the US. At times we disclosed what was in our minds as we wrote — this particular aspect of our collaboration is important, because we did not write blindly. The poem is more a result of a merging of minds rather than a serendipitous creation.

Whoever said "three's a crowd" never collaborated on a poem. Although having three different poets weighing in on each word was at times unwieldy, we came to an agreement about the success of each line fairly quickly.

After brainstorming for titles and reaching a consensus about closing the poem, we recorded the voice, and completed the video.

Watch the video at http://qarrtsiluni.com/2009/01/29/winding/

He's Created What I Have in Mind

Jeff Fioravanti and Tom Sheehan

Jeff Eff's *Lily Pond Transit*

He declares hidden sets for me, pastel passage, same seat I have sat,
though different set of eyes, wondering where the spring, summer
and winter's at. The hidden fires of fall have declined, flame without
smoke, though fire's heart was born in stem, stalk and sprig in spring;
fall leaf and limb all flame, so cindered. Summer brazier on sunlit girl,
a sylph from diving board, who October wears a soft yellow sweater,
a skirt to match, who when the fire's lit, thinks the fall's the end of it.
Not sparks we hit, old ice houses in sheets of flame, wild sparks due
a mile away, heat enough for spring. Oh, yes, that's it. Back to spring.
He thinks perhaps I see canoes slipping off pickerel-like from LeHavre
or New London's watered pit, or a skater's pond-wide whitened trail
on year's first ice, twice black thunder leaping up the shore, and more,
the core of unheard music from olden noisy Odin's Valkyrie with baton
underfoot, a blade honed by youth got on. Younger you and your crew
have followed arcs and marks leave visible the volts of thundering bolts.
Oh, Lily Pond's never the same, takes aim for becoming done and gone
in seasonal's phenomenon. Yet Jeff tells me what it is, how he recollects
his past from where he paints beside the pond, and mine, for all of that.

Tom: I've been thinking of collaborating. Take a peek at Qarrtsiluni. Perhaps a Lily Pond scene, our first common ground, might realize something nice.

Jeff: Let me see what I can develop. We're on a short porch, submissions due by January 15th. Something of Lily Pond would be interesting. Let me see what comes.

Tom: I'll keep a log of messages to support the effort, a piece of the submission. There's free rein on the type of art. I wasn't thinking of drawing you away from your work, but thought a pass at some graphic image or painting would do. It would take both sides of the coin to get what might be acceptable.

Jeff: I went to the pond yesterday, walking in from Central Street along the river, to get some reference material. Will continue to search and see what develops.

Tom: Much of what I remember is in the attached, "Diamond-faced Lily Pond." When you have some time, take a look at it. Perhaps it'll touch something in you.

Jeff: We share the same sentiments. Yesterday, as I walked past the river and the bridge no longer there, I remembered walking the woods to Billy Mitchell's house or listening to highway traffic or staring at a winter evening's sky. I tried to imagine my mother's stories. The striking one is the Prentice boys saving her after a fall through the ice. I remember playing army with other kids, walking through after a football game, much later hiking to Martignetti Liquors and sharing a brew under the summer sky. I've watched the pond shrink and yet remain a treasure. Now I search for the right image for those thoughts.

Tom: (Saw Jeff's pastel painting today, Lily Pond in fall colors, from below John Burns's house. He will send me a pix. Lovely.)

Jeff: I shoot all my artwork with slide film, liking the way it captures images. Some background here: the painting was done in "en plein air" and is a pastel painting on watercolor board, toned to burnt sienna, of the area by the swing sets. I removed the houses in the background, trying for an original look. Rolling clouds were a challenge, occasionally blotting out the sun, playing havoc with the color scheme. This piece was created during the morning. The submission page doesn't say what DPI or format the image should be. I've made this 300 dpi. The size of the piece is 7×9.

Tom: (Received email with the painting and was transported.)

Jeff: You've captured my thoughts, what I tried to catch in my painting, same seat, same scene, different but intertwined. I thought of trodden leaf, faded footsteps, seasons gone by, solitude, visiting old friends, sounds of hockey, plop of fishing lures, rustle of leaves, how we all eventually pass on, but still the seat and the place remain. I thought how you and I share a thread, tied together to this place. I thought of loneliness sitting there, like leaves lost from the trees. I think in many ways you've captured what I tried to capture. Different memories, different dreams, same place. I sit here grinning warmly, satisfied.

Miracle Fish

Karla Huston and Cathryn Cofell

Place the cellophane fish in your palm
and wait. Let him warm to you,
find your cradle, the curve of your inner
nature. His actions will tell your fortune.
A moving head means jealousy,
a finicky tail means indifference.
And so you unfold through all his stirrings.

He bucks and twists in my hand,
nearly falling over himself to get me right.
But every time I open either palm
to this red minnow, he turns a different story.
Today, I am tail over mouth: fickle.
Yesterday, his fin-flick called me passion.
Sometimes late at night, he flips
all the way and claims that I am false.

I want to know how seven seconds
and a sliver of head-shop plastic
know me so well when my own
husband holds me all night, his whole body
cloaked over mine, his whole body absolutely
still? According to the key, his silence says
I am the dead one.
So tell me, Miracle Fish,
how much of me is approximately true,
which scarlet fortune do I believe?

Process notes

Cofell and Huston have written collaboratively off and on since 2000. They have worked mostly in Exquisite Corpse by email as well as in person but have also experimented with assignments controlled around a theme. Perhaps most successful has been allowing each other to write within abandoned poems and allowing this process to create something new. Because they value friendship and respect each other as writers, they've established some working rules that seem to eliminate potential problems. For example, they agree to revise only their own lines and abandon a poem that doesn't seem to be working. Rather than feeling that their own voices have been muted by writing together, they feel as if they've created a third voice that is quite freeing and fun.

Inspired by one of those trinket-shop, cellophane fish, this poem is the result of Karla writing a poem that was stuck. She wasn't sure where to go with it and had more or less given up. So she "gave it away" to Cathryn who wrote inside the poem and around it, adding her own flourishes and took it somewhere new. Then we looked at it together, tweaking line by line, but only making changes to which we both agreed. We think the finished piece is greater than the sum of its parts.

westward ho

Leslie F. Miller and Jennifer König

she pauses by the mirror,
sees a wrinkle in her fabric,
a curlicue of fear.
she fingers a trinket,
broken badge
on a chain held taut,
then prinks her face up pretty,
prominent mandibular aside
(she sees no remedy
for that bad bone).
a trick of the light, she thinks,
placing the luminaria on the sill.
hers was a temporal display.
yanked back to the now
with a colloquial howdy from behind,
she sees his face, a panorama
of wild west wink and ten-gallon charm
crenellated maw of smiling spurs.
one swish, and she is in his arms,
a dime-store bargain at twice the price.

Process notes

she fingers a trinket

Leslie laid some procedural ground rules.

1.) We would write two stanzas, one of eight lines, the other of twelve, for the eight nights of Hanukkah and the twelve days of Christmas. Form is arbitrary in the end, though.

2.) With a total of 20 lines, we'd each contribute ten words that must be used, in any order, one per line. I would use one from her list; she one from my list.

3.) We would each start a stanza and finish a stanza.

In the end, we'd edit the poem — decide on punctuation, lines that don't fit, etc. This way, it is an entirely 50/50 collaboration, right down to the title — we thought of the same one. Even the lines we wrote on our own were written with the other's word.

When we were satisfied with the poem, Jennifer suggested we take a shot to go with it and post it here. We did not discuss the shot beforehand.

a colloquial howdy from behind

Below, the words we used.

Jen's Words

west
trinket
luminaria
temporal
swish
taut
colloquial
bone
fabric
mandibular

Leslie's Words

panorama
curlicue
remedy
pause
prink
badge
crenellation
yank
bargain
trick

Icon in a Green Walnut Shell

Harold Rhenisch and Daniela Elza

the sound of wind shifting stones, slowly,
over centuries, is how a woman walks

the land.   a sound you can only hear
when you grow   still

between   the thud of heart
(the blue vein of the horizon)

and the night   (the red veil
of the lung).

a man is how we silence trees. the sound
of the wind shifting stones

is an avalanche   in the white sheet of
the tongue. is how a child grasps

wheat fields, scratches stars down
from the dark.   We use words

borrowed from old countrysides.   look up.
their meanings as if they are vials

full of nostrum brewed by   no one.   the rest
is the way a   man speaks

trees,   that blossom into houses. then prays.
the green veil of the   fingers

plucking the sky from its   roots
is how a woman listens. slowly, over centuries

is how   plutonium blossoms in the core
of our bones. is how a child gasps The

call of the raven startles us
into a story,   where we are not

the beginning, and words
not the end   or the telling

but what we break open.   in our half-lives.
what we share, what we crouch to eat.

on the edge of night

Process notes

This process started years ago, when I (Harold) used to climb my walnut tree in the mountains of British Columbia and shake down walnuts which I picked up from the fall chrysanthemums, and, far away in Bulgaria, I (Daniela) was falling in love with a walnut tree in my grandmother's yard, staining my fingers on their husks, eating the milky fruit inside.

After that, things were quiet for many years, we both became better writers while working with Daniela's poems, and began to wonder how we could apply what we had learned. We discussed working out the parameters of a new method of teaching, but it was difficult to get beyond the roles of teacher and student, although we were neither. I (Harold) got the idea that the next step might be to write poems together, without selves, to write them as shared objects. I conceived of them as dramas. W>i<e made a couple attempts that went nowhere, as the process began with poems that appeared finished and the work of breaking them, so they could be reformed, was more difficult than w<i>e anticipated. Thus invitation was already there.

Then Daniela found a line in a story of Harold's in The Malahat Review, quickly added a few verses to it, and sent it Harold's way, suggesting he mutate the signature.

I (Harold) had fun with it, picked up on the rhythms (I) Daniela had set up, modified them, depersonalized adjectives, and ran with it as far as I could.

W>i<e both continued this process of shuffling and movement, and within two days of tossing it back and forth w<i>e had a poem that was larger than w>i<e were (was). Most of what was exchanged between us was the poem back and forth. Not much else in terms of explanations. Now that w<i>e have found a way to balance form with improvisation, w>i<e will be writing many more.

Entente Cordiale: An Ekphrastic Exchange

Anna Dickie and Lucy Kempton

After Silence

I dream of waking where neon
blooms, and nightsong is a siren
blare or the rattle of a tram.

I fear a life spent in a gloomy
house, surrounded by a broody
wood, tending a fickle orchard

Poem by Anna, photographs by Lucy, mutated by Anna

and shady gardens without end.
I know forest paths like these,
and how well women come

to tread them. I don't know
what bound me to you.
Lost in the dark I stood still,

said nothing. So forgive me,
as I set you free — of me.

Goatskin, goatson

Hung from a nail in the parching sun, a passion flower
clings and climbs around the post. Forget scripture,
though my sides and seams, once sealed with pitch,
crack and craze, take me, fill me with new wine.

Carry me over the hills and groves, to the summer pastures,
the uplands where once I sprang on rocks and grazed,
to remember, once more, nibbling twigs of myrtle and olive,
bitter and fragrant.

*Poem by Lucy,
photograph by Anna,
mutated by Lucy, with
help from Anna*

Drink from me there, and I'll show you, from out of the wine,
dark joy, and bright sorrow, pride and falling from grace,
and pity, and the final emptying; a small kind of tragedy,
a sad drunk goat song.

Process notes

Anna Dickie writes:
Our entire collaboration took place by e-mail;
we've never spoken face-to-face or by phone.
Early on, by way of background, we had the
idea to write introductory biographies/impres-
sions of each other. These we've included at
the end.

I selected two images, one of a place and one
of a thing, for Lucy to respond to. And as Lucy
writes often about the countryside, I chose a
city shot for the place, as I wanted to see her
take on something urban.

I like to use a Lensbaby lens for cityscape, as
it provides interesting distortions of buildings
and people, so my "place" image was a duo-
toned shot of the Playfair steps in Edinburgh, a
long set of well-worn steps that lead up to the
Old Town.

Lucy was more generous than me in choosing
images for me to respond to, sending me five
images: a moving carousel, a French country
house and grounds, a stack of old terracotta
floor tiles, a war memorial, and a bride and
groom walking in a beauty spot to have photographs taken.

The "thing" choice was a black-and-white shot
of an old goatskin wine sack hanging from a
post on a farm high up in the levadas of Madeira. (Country people there still use goatskins
to store wine.)

I was immediately drawn to the country house shot — black and white and beautifully framed by a sinister ivy-covered gate — and the colour image of the wedding couple.

I then thought of Wendell Berry's poem, "Country of a Marriage," which I think is a rather smug, comfortable, male view of a marriage. And that got me wondering if I could subvert Lucy's two photographs into a single image that had the feel of a French film still, and then write a poem in the voice of a bride that had something of the mood of the photograph. I tackled the images first, but try as I might I couldn't get the couple at the angle I wanted on the path, until I had the idea of flipping the whole country house shot horizontally using Photoshop. This worked really well, as it put the gate pillar on the left opening up the scene, and when the couple were added in it put the bride on the groom's right, making her seem the more powerful figure who was doing all the talking while he took on a rather hangdog expression.

After that I applied some dodging and burning to the image, to bring out the light on the trees and then applied some digital "film grain" to make the shot more atmospheric.

With the poem I borrowed some of the word choices from the original to create a completely new poem about a woman whose thoughts about being with this man, in this place only crystallise on the day of their marriage.

I'll leave it for Lucy to say what she thought about the result.

Lucy Kempton writes:
I read Anna's poem first, and was intrigued by how she seemed to have woven the narrative possibilities of the two photos together. Then I looked at the picture in the attachment and was astonished — it gave me a shiver like seeing a ghost! The figures sat disturbingly in the scene, but at the same time seemed to belong there. Yet I had never envisaged combining the two images in such a way. I was struck too by how the spike in the gate seemed to be about to impale the woman, like pinning a butterfly.

Then I read the Wendell Berry poem, which I

didn't know. I also thought it had a somewhat self-satisfied tone, an assumption of knowing what the woman concerned thought and felt, of the unarguable universality of his own perception, though of course my reading of it was by then coloured by Anna's poem! But I was very taken with the "he-said-she-said" character of her response, the piquant counterpoint of the woman's terser, diverging point of view, the sadness of the voice, and the atmosphere of place it captures, the "broody woods" and "fickle orchards."

While I think Anna's poem and the composite image she made can each stand alone and without reference to the Wendell Barry poem, the synthesis of the three elements makes for something more. I'm delighted with how she saw the potential in the two images together, then drew on a further outside source to make such a clever, moving piece.

Anna:
My second choice was Lucy's image from Normandy of some old terracotta floor tiles left stacked outside in some scrubby grass. I worked with this to create a text overlay on the image, a short poem in the form of sequential questions, rather in the style of the nursery rhyme 'The house that Jack built'.

However, though pleased with what I produced, we eventually felt that both of our secondary pieces, the "Floor Tiles" and the "Playfair Steps," made the overall submission unwieldy, so we concentrated our efforts on the major poem and picture combinations, and decided to submit the others, both in text/image overlay form, to Postal Poetry.

Lucy:
Having already received Anna's photos for me to work with, I noted she had selected one image of a place and one of a thing, so I tried to follow suit. I tended to favour black and white in my choices, though not exclusively, perhaps rather influenced by knowing that Anna has a fondness for it. Unable to narrow down to just two, I sent two "places" and three "things." Among these were the black and white photo of a chateau in the countryside hereabouts, which, with its heavy flaking iron gates, shady drive and general shabbiness has always epito-

mised for me a kind of melancholy hostility and otherness (the owner has, I learned later, something of a reputation for misanthropy and reclusiveness).

Then I added the odd, quickly taken shot of the bride and groom in formal wedding dress, whom I'd seen being photographed in an area of quite lonely, empty coastal marshland, a place which seemed a strange, slightly surreal choice for this. I had kept the picture, feeling it had some potential I couldn't quite identify, and threw it in at the last minute for Anna as a kind of wild card. I'm glad I did.

Anna:
I'm glad that we just sent each other the images with little by way of explanation. We didn't agree to do this, it was just how things worked out, but it meant that we were free to interpret the images any way we pleased.

I also think it's interesting that despite trying to coax each other towards other ideas/images our strongest pieces came out of the subjects that are closest to our hearts — and maybe that is a useful lesson to learn, that you can challenge yourself with new things, but ultimately you will always come back to what truly moves/interests you.

Lucy:
Anna sent me the photographs of the Madeiran goatskin, an extraordinary object the like of which I hadn't seen before, and the mysterious one of the Playfair steps in her beloved Edinburgh with a shadowy figure at the top. I printed the photographs so that I could keep them around for a time and look at them frequently, and mull over the ideas and associations they suggested. The prevalent things in my mind about goatskins were the biblical reference to not putting new wine in them, together with a curiosity as to how they were made watertight enough to hold wine at all, and, by assonance, the word "goatsong," the translation of the Greek word tragoidia — tragedy, the origin of which remains opaque. I did a little research, and eventually a combination of ideas surrounding landscape, tragedy, wine and the life, death and final fate of a goat produced the final poem.

Unable to settle, I also attempted a more formal version in two Sicilian octaves; I thought Sicily seemed quite appropriate for the subject even though the goatskin was from Madeira! I sent them both to Anna, who chose the first version, which I was generally happier with too.

After she had read it, Anna, who knows I enjoy making double or multi-exposure collages, tentatively suggested a wine stain might add something to the goatskin image to go with the poem. She was a little apologetic about leading me, but I was cheerfully open to the suggestion, and set about sloshing some ropey old cooking Chianti onto various light coloured surfaces (no oenophile sensibilities were hurt in the making of this picture). I made the collage using Picasa's multi-exposure collage function, then tweaked the levels somewhat, still in Picasa. However, it was still rather faint and had lost detail, so Anna, who always knows how much more can be got out of an image without ever compromising its integrity, further improved it using curves in Photoshop. She even made a funky little grid of the wine stain and the Chianti bottle photos I sent her later.

The intriguingly named Playfair Steps sent me off on a trail of research on Edinburgh, which triggered some associated memories. The short poem arising from that, like Anna's roof tiles, we removed from the final cut, and, in text-on-picture form, submitted elsewhere, as mentioned.

Anna:
I was walking down from a long levada walk towards a welcome drink when I spotted this poor old goatskin hanging from one of the posts they use to support the grape vines that surround every homestead on the island. This particular homestead was almost in ruins and a passion flower had crept in and taken over the post and most of the surrounding area. I knew right away it would make a great black and white shot, particularly due to the texture in the cracked skin and the worn string. Our driver for the day picked up a new goatskin full of wine to deliver to relatives, and it was much less appealing, as it looked and felt like a large stuffed intestine.

I was touched and amazed by the rigour of Lucy's research, and the number of ideas that my image evoked. I also liked how she tapped into the timelessness and the history of the object, which was what struck me when I saw it. And when I saw the finished pieces I was forcibly struck by just how well she'd captured the life, death and spirit of the goat.

I also liked the lovely circularity of her idea of the goatskin going back to the mountains.

I did feel guilty about suggesting the wine stain, as I wasn't sure if it was acceptable for me to suggest a further mutation of Lucy's initial mutation. Perhaps I suggested it because I was happily cutting up her pictures, but I think it was these words: "the final emptying; a small kind of tragedy" in the last stanza of her piece that made me feel it would be both poignant and shocking to see something in colour, suggesting both the goat's blood and the wine, applied to the black and white image of the sack.

Drafting — how we both work

Lucy:
I prefer to start most writing with pen and paper. Keyboard and screen always, initially, present too many barriers: mediocre keyboard skills, a tendency to be distracted by things like e-mails and internet, guilt about being glued to a screen too long. On the whole, I simply find pen and paper more sympathetic, a safe, unjudgemental place to simply scribble and scrub out whatever comes to mind. I also like pen and paper from a sensory point of view; I have cheap, usually spiral notebooks of different sizes and carry them about, on my knee on the sofa, on the breakfast table, the kitchen counters, in bags and pockets, along with fine-liner pens. I gather there are those who develop similar intimate, companionable relations with their laptops, but I can't.

However, there comes a point when the sheer volume of dog-eared, palimpsestuous drafts becomes unmanageable:

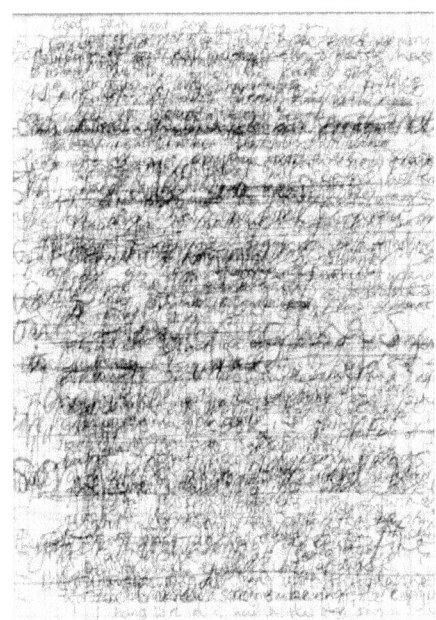

(Just kidding! This is a multi-exposure collage, a product imitating a process, but it gives an impression.)

And then it's time to sift them all out,

attempt something approaching what I want to achieve, get it onto the computer, and then tinker around some more: punctuation, line breaks, word changes… One has to stop somewhere.

It occurs to me that with more and more writing taking place exclusively on electronic media, the process becomes increasingly fugitive and invisible, so attempts like this to record it necessarily become artificial re-creations after the fact. We have become aware in this collaboration that a blow-by-blow, unedited record of the process is neither desirable nor really possible. Probably this doesn't matter. I see it as a little like turning over a piece of weaving to see the reverse side, with its knots and ends and rough bits; you see something of the finished process, not in linear form in the order it was achieved, but dotted about over the surface you don't normally see.

In addition, on this project, we submitted everything we wrote to one another for editing and suggestions. I have enjoyed this process, including — perhaps most of all — the parts which we ended up leaving out.

Anna:
I too usually start with a paper draft, however I'm not so organised as to have spiral notebooks or favourite pens. No, my approach is more a case of grabbing the gas bill envelope and some scuzzy pencil from the kitchen drawer to scribble down a line or phrase that's popped into my head as I haul clothes from the washing machine or peel the spuds.

However, for this project I seemed to go straight for the computer, perhaps because I was re-reading the Wendell poem online, or perhaps because working online made me feel a little more connected to the images, the project and to Lucy.

I must admit to really enjoying working with Lucy's images, as I felt much more detached than when I edit my own photographs, where I'm already burdened with knowing where the shot was taken, or the mood I was in on the day, or the idea I was trying to convey.

I have also enjoyed our e-mail contact. We both blog, but this project has made it quite obvious just what a presentation of self a blog is. Correspondence, even by e-mail, is much more 3-D.

We probably should have fleshed out more ground rules before we started, but from my standpoint the serendipity of this project has only added to the process.

It's been fun working with Lucy, and I just hope that shows in our results.

Lucy:
Although our ideas for photos and poem responses came quite easily, it seemed to take a while for us to tune in to each other on how to go about presenting the process, so we digressed and produced quite a lot of tangential stuff not featured here, which was fun anyway. We gossiped, even though we were only communicating by e-mail, which used up time, but, again, was enjoyable. We like each other and each other's work, which meant perhaps we were reluctant to criticise, chivvy, make alternative suggestions, or weed out anything the other produced, though we did do this eventually, and perhaps makes us slip into

mutual admiration mode when talking about one another, which is sincere but I hope not too off-putting.

It's difficult knowing when to stop adding and adjusting, more so than when working alone, because of the compulsion to keep responding.

The other problem is practical and technical, unwanted mutation arising from using different softwares, copying and pasting etc, giving rise to a ragtag array of different fonts and lost line breaks, which needed continual, time-consuming tinkering with. Should have used a Google document…

Our biographies of each other:

Lucy on Anna

Anna recently noted that being lately detoxed from an aromatase inhibitor drug, used in the treatment of breast cancer, provided welcome relief from years of low spirits and insomnia following treatment for Stage 3 breast cancer. I was somewhat surprised.

This was the woman I first encountered when I read Peeling Onions, the narrative series she wrote in haiku, which related her personal experience of cancer with strength, dignity and honesty; the woman who produces beautiful, distinctive, bold photos that win prizes and a chapbook of poems that people buy; who participates in poetry readings and workshops and exhibitions; who badgers me to get my photo-editing skills up to scratch and sends me the wherewithal to do it; who undertakes what I would consider to be extreme gardening projects (she once offered to come and stay with me in exchange for cutting all our hedges and teaching me how to use Photoshop properly — I nearly took her up on it but didn't want to be shown up); who travels to interesting places, supports other cancer sufferers, has a husband, a son, a dog, who finds and shares wonderful videos on YouTube (the Phil Collins gorilla was a memorable one)… I could go on.

So, if she's been doing all that in a state of depressed sleep deprivation, what's she going to be doing now she's feeling better?

I soon found out.

"Do you want to send each other some photos and write about them for qarrtsiluni?" she asked.

"O.K."

Two minutes later the photos arrived.

Several days later, after much poring and indecision, I sent her some of mine.

Two minutes later…

Anna on Lucy
I'm not sure how long I've been dipping into Lucy's blog to read and enjoy her photo essays on life in the French countryside and much else besides.

But I keep returning because Lucy has the rare gift of managing to look at the world afresh each day, enjoying all the small and intimate pleasures it has to offer — like seeing a friend's new baby thrive, and a water lily bud break, and then combining these two images into one shot of a lovely little waterbaby.

Even when things get difficult and challenging, like recently when Tom, Lucy's partner, was in hospital, she still manages to record the facts in an open, gentle and genuine way — and this is a real tonic in a world where people seem overly ready to bemoan their lot.

Lucy's openness to life can be clearly seen and enjoyed in her recent exploration of the ancient poetic form of the ghazal; and some of her pieces have been published in The Ghazal Page, the online journal devoted to that subject.

And I know I'm not alone in liking her work; many others enjoy it too, especially the Handbook for Explorers, a cycle of 50 sonnets by Joe Hyam, matched beautifully with Lucy's highly interpretive images.

So when the qarrtsiluni submission call for "Mutating the Signature" dropped into my inbox, I immediately thought of Lucy and wondered if she would be willing to work with me.

In retrospect, 1984 made a fine sausage—

Arlene Ang and Valerie Fox

Our house was a pirate ship that changed colors
the further south we went

Once we had to pretend to wash a neighbor's dog
so we could wash ourselves and use the dog shampoo

The few times I had to attend school
I occupied a corner with my shadow

Mother told us we were not her dogs
For a dollar we held in our urine for more than eight hours

I eavesdropped on banal conversations
with a homeland kind of insecurity

To throw off our creditors we, the children,
were given fictitious names and religions

I counted on winning a pig or two at the county fair
even though I hated pork with navy beans

I sat on the stairs all night
and pretended I was John Hurt

Market day, previously a day reserved for apples,
became an occasion to watch roadkill from a moving truck

I almost acquired a wooden leg after our run-
in with the revolving door

I seriously considered renting out my mind
for a few dollars and some hospital cafeteria food

It was annoying when those insane people
used to smack us for being insane

Mother followed us around the grocery
when she wouldn't let us stay out in the car

Father, on the other hand, lost his marriage licence and later,
all his teeth to a gum disease.

He rarely spoke
except to say give me some private or

I'm counting on the lottery even
though I never get the ticket

There's a lot to do
until you fall asleep

It was infuriating how "uncle" littered
his gossip with my phrases about him watching

My list of infuriating things grew
by yards in my unsteady hand

Practical jokes of yore and yonder:
dribble cups, classified ads, glue in strange places

On another occasion the whole community turned
out in force to shun me

It was summer, yes
We were the last 43 pages torn

out of a novel and no one
could afford a happy ending

Process notes

Arlene writes: The title is a line from a poem in our book, *Bundles of Letters Including A, V and Epsilon* (Texture Press, 2008). We wanted to work towards real collaborative writing as opposed to writing poems based on each other's poems. It was written as part of our survival tactics during a 30-poems-for-30-days marathon in ITWS, an online writers' community. The process: One of us would initiate a poem (5-8 lines per day), and then we just kept hitting the ball back and forth. Afterwards we jumble our lines and edit, edit, edit.

OY YO

Luigino Solamito and John M. Bennett

Luigino Solamito

JOHN M. BENNETT

1 3 SET. 2008

Seurat to Continuity

Jed Myers and Priya Keefe

Hills hills miles miles
empty of us   Each

under our 4am blankets
in our funnels   of breath

nearer to the dark
glass bottom of emptiness itself

Deeper than the glass we peered through
at dinner under   the clicking of conversation

No conversation   now
where a goblet of breath empties

down a gullet   red with swallowed distress
into the cavernous   never-lit   void

There   an undiscovered aurora
borealis   emits   its lonely

sheen   onto the dark sea
starry   acidic   deep

infinite and intimate   where
we meet

It's no farther from my house to yours
than an arc inside

a star's pinpoint   of light
against the clear dark of tonight

And still   nearer
the distance between us

Under the roads   hills   breath
is a cat's cradle of hollow fibers

where once is forever   once
we've touched   We're the sparks

arcs of urgency   to connect
the dots   Seurat   to continuity

end the awful space
inside   between us

Filled glass   unfilled
lungs   dots in the lightdark spectrum

white   of our eyes
black   of the room

We're blind pixels   of a story
we can't tell   or see

Without effort   our lungs fill again
Starlight soaks the hills   seeps
in   reaches us   here

Process notes

Jed writes: When Dana invited me to give this venture a try, I thought immediately of Priya, with whom I've collaborated in various ways many times in recent years — we've written poems back and forth, I've performed aloud with her some poems for two voices, backed her up with guitar while she recited or sang, she's helped me host poetry gatherings… and our sensibilities, as persons and poets, are deeply resonant. So I had no hesitation in asking her to join me in the emergence of a poem for Dana's potential editorial delight.

Upon agreement from Priya, some weeks back now, I sent her a "seed" of something, a short segment starting "hills hills miles miles…" with the idea she'd respond by adding, altering, subtracting, reacting — who knew?! I knew I was addressing, in a kind of gut language, the reality of what separates us across the landscape of space and time, inviting her to wrestle with this with me. And she did — she added to it, and then I added to that, and then in the several backs and forths of it by email attachment exchange, followed by meeting over coffee and phone conversation, we elaborated and shaped and modified this little piece that seems to express a shared feeling about our lives being too separate, where distances that manifestly get in the way of more abiding connection are inescapable yet at the same time not present in our depths, not actual at the deepest levels of personal truth, but O how we do struggle with the distances, the discontinuities, the hills and miles, as our more overt conscious usual selves. We sense there is a deeper stratum, a "cats cradle" of interconnections, between, among, any and all who've ever really touched, been moved or shaken, loved, changed or been changed, but this sense is usually remote. The poem hopes to bring this a bit closer.

The process of the poem — and a way to wonder about its success as a poem, I think — is a struggle toward resolution of an irresolvably dual truth. We are at once in the actual and the experiential worlds — the world of the hills and of the "hollow fibers/where once is forever" — and it may well be that at some fundamental level deeper than conscious experience, "under the roads," an ineradicable continuity abides. This is a wish, a longing, a conjecture or intuition, and one pole in the tense polarity explored by us organically in the poem.

Priya writes: We didn't discuss topic or approach beforehand. My partner Jed started the poem, wrote eight lines and emailed it to me. I wrote eight lines, emailed it back. We each took another turn and then seemed to agree, without discussion, that the first draft was complete. Although I did not state that I had written a conclusion, he responded with an email that indicated he also felt the first draft was complete. My favorite part of this process was watching the mystery unfold.

We agreed to each take a pass at editing before we got together via phone or in person. I edited lightly, trying to stay true to the original version and not insert too much of my voice via editing. I felt there was only so much further I could take the poem without discussing its meaning with Jed.

We met in a coffee shop on a rainy Saturday afternoon. I brought a copy of each version of the poem: the original, Jed's edited version, and my edited version. Knowing it can be informative and inspirational to hear one's work read by someone else, I read aloud Jed's edited version, then he read aloud my edited version. Then we discussed areas where we felt meaning or language was unclear. New understandings evolved through this process! Through reading and discussion, we came up with another version that was more lucid and balanced our two voices.

I think the next time I embark on a process of writing a poem collaboratively, I would like to try discussing an approach beforehand. Although challenging to find and integrate a balance between both voices in the writing and editing we did apart, the discussion and editing we did together was playful and energized the poem.

Wood for Your Fire

12 Measures of Interest

When your faith is a desert, under darkest of skies
When you wander empty tombs in the wind,
When all your rivers have gone silent, and your streams have run dry
When your roads have all come to an end,

> *Chorus:*
> I'm the wood for your fire, what you need in this land
> Of prophets and poets, scratching psalms in the sand. [repeat]

When grace is a desert, under hottest of suns
When your love is as bare as the trees,
When there's nothing in sight, of a swift, clearing dawn,
When your death is a morning to me,

> [Chorus]

When heaven is a wasteland, under clouds without rain,
Your song is the sweetest of springs.
Like you I have wandered, like you I was lost,
Now all that you need I will bring.

> [Chorus]

When your faith is a desert, under darkest of skies
When you wander empty tombs in the wind,
When all your rivers have gone silent, and your streams have run dry
When your roads have all come to an end,

> [Chorus]

I'm the wood for your fire, the sandals for your street
The heart of your desire, the stones beneath your feet.
I'm the honey for your hunger, the well for your thirst
The roar of the thunder, the breaker of the curse.

Lyrics by Melissa Lamberton and Ken Lamberton
Music by 12 Measures of Interest: Melissa, Ken, Bill Devinney, Eric Cross, Celia Major, and Pat Kelly

Listen to the .mp3 at http://qarrtsiluni.com/2009/02/16/wood-for-your-fire/

Ken writes: My daughter Melissa and I have been writing music recently, which my band 12 Measures of Interest then performs at church — a Lutheran church with a rock-and-roll band. The end result, however, is really a composition from six people since each member of the band contributes his/her own artistic flare. Our first original song, "Wood for Your Fire," was first performed a few months ago. The recording isn't professional, just a couple of microphones set up in front of us, but it's not too bad.

Melissa first came up with the idea in a "love" poem she wrote that had the line "I'm the wood for your fire" and some other phrases like "prophets writing in the sand." She and I then began playing with the lyrics as I worked up a rudimentary melody on my acoustic guitar. It took several months of hashing out the final song, working from the "wood for your fire" theme — Melissa was very particular about every word. She didn't want the final result overtly "religious" and wanted to maintain the original love poem. Once we had the lyrics and basic melody, I shared the song with my music group, who added their own quality. I play bass, so I turned the guitar rhythm over to Bill Devinney, who also added a harmony line. Eric Cross developed the percussion and additional harmony. Celia Major came up with the wonderful high vocal harmony while Pat Kelly on lead guitar chose the slide bar to add his own particular flavor to the end result.

Melissa writes: This song began life as a poem. The line "I'm the wood for your fire" stayed with me long after the poem was finished — this idea of a love so pure it consumes itself to keep another warm. Love strips you down to the essentials, so I wanted the scene to be a desert — a place where simple necessities become an abundance. The words changed as we fit them to music, but that sense of haunting desolation remained. It seemed impossible to play in anything but a minor key.

Arena Chapel

Greer DuBois and Wendy Vardaman

"Follow
me to Florence?" my
master asked, spying my sheep.
Just ten, I said, "Yes,
I will."

"I will
not forget." "You will,"
old Scrovegni scoffs, then turns
away. "Please. Restore
my name."

"I will
teach," Cimabue
promised, "painting." "I'll finish this
first. "Please. Step out of
my light."

"My name
is in your hands," he
exchanged with the gold. Giotto
smocked the son's orders
and tears.

The light
dimming, he can still
picture when their forms began
to jell: flowing gowns
and tears.

Enter-
ing the fresco, he
presents his gift to Mary.
The father doesn't
follow.

Process notes

We began writing this poem at the end of a semester in Florence, having spent several months
traveling and studying the amazing medieval and renaissance fresco cycles throughout Italy. Both
poets with an interest in visual art, Greer (the daughter) and Wendy (the mother) studied and wrote
about these paintings individually over the months. When qarrsiluni's call for collaborative pieces
came out, we thought that the subject of fresco would be exciting to take on, since fresco is itself a
collaboration among many artists — masters and apprentices, sometimes over decades and among
more than one master. Although the Sistine Chapel in Rome is probably the most famous example
of these artworks, the earlier, more intimate Arena Chapel of Padua, by Giotto, may be the most
moving, and after much discussion, we agreed that we would like to try writing about it.

Both of us entered into the project with larger artistic ideas that we wanted to explore through the
collaborative project. Greer, who had previously been moaning about conventional ideas about the
place of the artist within a work and art as a whole, looked on the project as a way to challenge cur-
rent ideas about poets as individualistic "loners."

Meanwhile, Wendy wanted to create a form that would somehow capture and imitate the way
that individual paintings in a fresco cycle stand on their own as narratives, but connect with the

other paintings to create a larger story, sometimes playing off pieces painted above, below, or across from each other. After some thought, she came up with the individual, syllabic stanza units used in "Arena Chapel," which she called giottos after the painter that inspired them. These units fit together architecturally, one beginning with the same two syllables that end its predecessor, reflecting the multi-voiced, collaborative nature of this project. Although we chose to put the giottos of this poem together in the round, any number of alternative spaces, or chapels, could be created this way, and in fact, the poem already does continue in a number of other directions.

We each wrote three of the individual stanzas in this piece, beginning with a stanza of Wendy's that was pulled out of a sample cycle she composed to illustrate the form to Greer. After deciding where to start, we divided up the remaining stanzas, and then worked together at several sittings to put them together and revise, commenting on each other's words and characters, enjoying the sometimes serendipitous interplay of opposite lines, and actively working to create a unified story about two father/son pairs: Cimabue and Giotto, a master and apprentice, and the two Scrovegnis, immortalized both by Giotto's chapel and by Dante in the Divine Comedy. The brevity of the form we agreed to use, as much as the collaboration, shaped our work. Both of us found the form pushed us toward saying certain things in fairly telegraphic ways and prevented us from saying others; we had to keep renegotiating with each other the direction the narrative would take, how that would happen, and which individual giottos did not fit our shared vision. We have also talked about the possibilities of the form in performance with more than one voice, and would like to develop multiple ways of reading/delivering these pieces as we continue working on them.

What's displayed here is a section of what, we hope, will eventually be a long poem that tells more of the story of the Arena (Scrovegni's) Chapel.

April 21 Rooftop Corpse

Paul Nelson and Rebecca Rose

Dad & me race up the elevator, wow
we're liable to see Tahoma's Columbia Crest
which is why, in all my wildest dreams I never thought
the sun knows you are not a teenager. You
are only a mist in this downpour of old strangers &
coffee table conversation & dusty apricot sky above the feed
store. Rooftop tiles, scattered through the windowpanes of justice,
plane lights brighter now that the sun has just set,
behind my shin splint lay an assortment of chocolatey flavors
like the top of the mountain throwing off spring clouds
or the nesting lion, awakened by the unfamiliar
noises of mad hit & run whistlers (whistle & run?) does
that make the puppies fight for the dogwood,
pink in the middle as clouds above the sunset blinded Cascades
or the cliff-ghasts might get you. Sleep well my child, or
you will watch the sun's fatal hurtle toward Japan
& realize that conga lines do exist; Clifford suits ARE
real,
    & determined as dusk — as the 150 — as
bricks in an open sort of way, like they weren't really there,
like old Tahoma pinking itself in muted lavender
just so, like all the evening's gray coming 2gether in 1 last burst of life.

Process notes

Paul writes: I wrote this as an Exquisite Corpse with my daughter Rebecca Rose, who was 13 at the time. I started with a line and continued with one word on the next line and folded the page over so she could not see anything but the one word I left for her. She did the same and we kept doing that until the end of the page. We recorded it at the studios of Auburn Community Radio, a project since canceled by the city. The rooftop is the Auburn Transit Center, a prison-like structure in downtown Auburn.

Writing these spontaneous poems, made popular by the surrealists, has been a fun way to pass time, document the moment and liberate full metaphoric activity as Andre Breton said about corpses. It allows for a truly organic process.

(Listen to the recording to hear which words were authored by whom. — Eds.)

Walking the Dogs Between Blizzards

Jessamyn Smyth and Anne Morrison Smyth

We walk, Gilgamesh and I, in preparation for the storm, twenty-five inches predicted.
Weeks below-zero and chilling winds solidified feet of snow already fallen; finally,
we can walk, skating across surface, only occasionally breaking
through. Gilly runs for sheer pleasure, throws himself forward, compensates with sheer velocity
for uncertainty of ground. He hurls his body into space, ahead, ever
ahead; plants his face suddenly into snow when he falls. He always comes up laughing, black fur dusted white, ears crinkled. This is what dogs do. We haven't walked enough lately;
snow too deep, crust too unreliable. I want to check on the beavers; it's been many weeks
since we've walked enough, in the back field and the woods by the stream. So we pass
Shalom's grave, a circle

of stones and a Japanese Maple surviving its second winter under heaps of snow. In a few months, the leaves will appear, scarlet, determined; yellow Narcissi will rise around the small tree and shout aggressive, happy color at the sky.

I invite the dead on my walks.

Gilly leaps

gratitude for our Northwesterly direction: behind the house, no stacks of wood to fuss with, no barns in which we do mysterious, officious human things

— sorting recycling, trying to get the damn mower to work —

no mailboxes to check, no boring cars for grocery shopping. To the Northwest, only trails; the ones I built with an ancient pair of garden shears, with bleeding, blistered hands while I grieved

Shalom

one tough, fibrous goldenrod stalk at a time,

for miles. Gilly bounces me repeatedly; I shove him off, but he doesn't stop, because I'm laughing. He knows that if a joke is funny the first time, it's even funnier the next

twelve times. He bounces, I laugh. He bounces,

I laugh. This is what dogs do.

We pass the old shed full of ancient farm equipment abandoned

by the hippies who built our place, the dairy farm family before them. Manure spreader, enormous steel carrot washer, old sleds, hay rakes with snapped handles, detritus from ramshackle greenhouse. The piles irritate. We have history enough

of our own, the interesting nature of the machines notwithstanding. They threw nothing away, ever, and everything left is broken, it weighs

a ton, it has to be dug out of the ground where they let it rot. One person's history;

another person's litter. We crunch through the stretch of trail that is marsh in spring; quails and pheasants nest there, sudden explosions of wings when we pass

the Christmas tree I dragged out to the property line, barricading the gap that invited hunters from the next farm. Gilly pees on it obligingly. Do not pass, no killing

here, the yellow snow says; this land is a territory belonging to the living, and to certain ghosts who are in that condition because of the likes of you: you who are not welcome

here with your gun and your beer can and your 'he came out of nowhere,

he died within minutes.' Here

is what dogs understand about time:

now. Or:

forever away from now. For a long time now I have walked, understanding what 'minutes' means to a dog who is dying,

alone.

Good boy, Gilly, I say. You have a nice, big pee right there. There is other pee around the Christmas tree, too; coyote, probably. Good coyotes. You mark that territory line. Mark it

well. We pause

at the choice of trails: left into the lower field and a short-cut to the beaver lodge, or straight toward the woods and stream, the long way 'round. The sumac canopy over the track into the woods beckons. Gilly looks at me, I look at him, and we break

for the woods. I lecture him: stay off the ice! He dances ahead, happily

ignoring me. At water's edge we see tracks and follow them to summer swimming hole, a convergence of streams. The small pool is frozen

now, swift waters bubble under ice. Dry Brook — named for miles of course that run underground — rises ice-cold, even in August, from the South. From the East,

Unadilla Brook runs warm through the swamp where trunks of dead trees rise gracefully, sometimes home

to eagles, herons, hawks. The tracks to the pool are large, but dusted with new snow; I can't tell who made them. Gilly tests the ice on the swimming hole, of course. I cringe

at creaks under his feet, his spread-wide toes, the light from below makes his webbing purple, his claws scrape for purchase. Convinced he will break through,

knowing he won't, I have to look away. I inspect the deepest mystery track, shout: 'I thought so!' Gilly hurries over to see

what's so exciting. 'Look,' I say, squatting down, pointing into large pad impressions and the outline of claws. 'Bear.'

Gilly plants his nose in the print, snuffles enthusiastically, inhales snow, sneezes it back out in an explosive

burst. His eyes water. I laugh, so he does too, ears crinkled, teeth half-revealed. He slaps my knee with his paw. Another good joke. This is what dogs do. Back through the woods, we skirt frozen stream, through maple and birch, under giant sycamores' thick, mottled, white trunks that rise like enormous

bones overhead. The lodge: a white heap at a bend in the stream. Ice unbroken around it; no tracks. Utterly silent. I wonder if it is warm

in there, under the ice and snow, in the muddy heat of bodies, snacking on stored branches. I guess it is, if you're a beaver.

We back away from the water: I don't like to intrude

at the lodge for long. We never see the beavers. We eavesdrop on summer cannonballs into water, felling of trees. We spy on smooth impressions of teeth everywhere. We admire amazing feats of engineering. We sneak glances at the living, as unobtrusively

as wonder allows. Above the lodge, the field we mow into a rough circle each summer is smooth, a white ballroom floor now. Gilly races to the center

and does a gavotte.

I used to come here with Shalom, renovating the abandoned house; before trails, before carrying furniture, boxes, his body, shovels to dig

his sudden grave. One day, Shalom and I stretched out in this wildish ring of field grass and milkweed, goldenrod, buttercups. We cloud-busted

together, for an hour; each chewing a piece of grass, on our backs. My arm around him. His head on my shoulder. His heart beat on my ribs. He smelled like grass,

Shalom did: even in winter, he had a grassy smell. I buried

my face in his fur during February cabin-fever and March doldrums and breathed deep summer. Gilly's smell is more floral, especially

when he's hot. His little armpits reek of flowers. His breath smells like mushroom soup. Right now, he has his first cold, so his nose is running

in the chill. The sky has a laden, leaden look all too familiar this winter. The light the soft-focus of imminent storm; edges softened, outlines blurred. It's warmer than it's been. Gilly and I follow tracks:

rabbit, then squirrel, chipmunk, deer. Rabbits and deer move in purposeful direction. Squirrels, chipmunks, mice, and dogs run in circles; they leave intricate swirls and knots of passage in the snow. We follow them all, winding

home past sleeping pear and cherry trees, cluster of pines, winter-berry brilliant red, we avoid hawthorn spike, drink land. Near the house, mulberry trees tangle messy and delightful. In summer, their berries turn bird guano the most alarming shade of fuchsia.

Shalom

goes and lies down in his grave. I wonder if it is warm in there, under the ice and snow, with his buried bed and his toys and his

emerging bones. I guess it is, if you're a ghost.

Ducking under tree boughs, treasure: 'Gilly!' I point. He looks up at the branch above my finger, where a single, frozen apple hangs. Apple,

one of the first English words he learned. He apple-dances every summer, tossing them over his back and leaping to catch them before they fall. His first autumn, he ate so much fermented fruit he got drunk. Dog Farm Apple Wine, we laughed, sitting at our fuchsia-streaked picnic table under mulberry.

Gilly sits for his apple. I jump

for it, hand him treasure he carries inside to thaw by the wood-stove. Later, he'll throw it around, smear it all over the couch and the floor. This

is what dogs do.

The storm arrives.

Chinese pear a lemon-summer burst on my tongue as outside the window fine, small flakes fly in diagonal sheets, the kind of snow

that isn't fooling around. Shalom's grave looks snug, and lonely, a white heap beyond glass walls. 'Come in

by the stove, love, if you want,' I say, through ice, through silence. Gilly, in his bed by the stove, looks up at me, bleary, already asleep. I wink at him. He goes back to sleep. The wood hoop is full, the covered shed stocked,

the stove-flue seems to be working again. I have candles, kindling. My favorite tea, cream. A working flashlight, another pear in the fridge. Vitamins, St. John's Wort, good dark coffee. Andres Segovia and Yo-Yo Ma,

split pea soup. We are settled,

in for the duration.

This is a walking collaboration. A collaboration of loss and witness. A mother handing down particular vision of love and love of place, a daughter handing it back transmuted through a different life and a separate sensibility.

This is what happened when the daughter said: help me keep this place, help me document its magic, the bones of it, the love buried here. This is what happened when the mother said: this is convergence, this is the blood of those we've lost on cold and frozen ground, this is some of what home and history is.

In January of 2007 and December of 2008, a mother and daughter walked in storms, bearing witness to loss and history through separate sensibilities.

It shouldn't be literal, necessarily, the daughter said. I mean, some of them might be, but not all — I want your interpretations of these words, your wholly separate vision of these themes as they exist for you. I know, the mother said. She doesn't like to talk about her photographs.

Look at that, the daughter said, on these walks.

I did, the mother answered.

Sad, fierce, true: something universal emerges through unshared particulars. A fundamentally shared experience of love, loss, and complicated history blows in sharp, diagonal sheets.

Debating Love

Tammy Ho Lai-ming and Reid Mitchell

PAT: How easily a sight of anything distracts a thought of a lover. I would, if I could, shut down the world.

FRANKIE: Don't talk crazy talk. You would shut down the generators that make the electricity that sends the lift to my flat? You would shut down the factories that make the sheets on which we lie? You would break the pipes that bring us water for us to brew tea and brush our teeth? The whole world is in a conspiracy to support our love.

Process notes

Tammy writes: Reid and I have been writing together for about three years now. We write what could be called "literary dialogues," although someone has commented that what we write are really "juxtaposed monologues" because the characters are often engaged in displaced conversations with themselves. We have also tried writing poems together and found the Villanelle works rather well. Since we live in two places, we write via the internet. Maybe one day we can write together for a longer period, sitting face-to-face.

"Debating Love" is a brief exchange which shows two people's collaborative effort to delude each other: Pat thinks the world is an obstacle to love, Frankie thinks the world is a confidant of love.

Rasterization

Elisa Gabbert and Kathleen Rooney

Words may not refer to anything, but if they do
they TV the objective world, white noising
over what might've been a nice view. On TV
membership has its privileges. In the library
I try to "get lost" in a "slender volume" but
the volume's too low. Sarcastic & bleak,
TV gets me. Even though TV doesn't know
how to love me. How I want it to watch me.
No one can keep track of my saccades,
but "Vide" can be used to direct a reader's
attention to what's on TV: basically
a forced obliteration of the landscape
w/ TV music. Allowing yourself to be used
is the best way to be used. Shibboleths
issue forth from the muted TV.

Process notes

Kathleen and Elisa have been collaborating on poems since February of 2006. All collaboration
has taken place via email while Elisa has been living in Boston and Kathleen has been living in
Provincetown, Tacoma, and now Chicago. They tend to kick off each round of collaboration by
deciding to work in a particular form, either a pre-existing one such as a sonnet, or one of their own
devising, such as a backwards poem. They usually compose line by line, with each of them reserving
the right to veto or call a do-over on her collaborator's contribution.

in the trade

Peter Schwartz and Colette Jonopulos

I've been collecting
ghosts, stamps, pins
my coins of doubt

even though all they'll
buy are more ghosts, real
only in the way

that small things
can be, our imperfect
worlds hung up

on tired clothes
lines.

-

the girls joke that soon
I'll need a second room
that no one

should need this many
memories, so I pinch my
arm between

waltzes to be with
them, they're kind
and I can.

-

so here I am
another pair of pearled
hips at 3:00 A.M.

praying in the fickle
manner of soldiers for
the sphinx to open

his wavelength
in my skull.

-

can you see me?
I'm prone as a telephone
trading gridlocked

bodies for infinite
rows of dreaming

awake but never
more than six feet
from my bed.

-

I'm pretty in this —
my little prison
of the obvious

the visitations
have changed, they're
threadbare

like the house
negligee I wear
and don't

like anything left
out in the animal
kingdom.

-

in the end, even
the power of my
nakedness

is denied; I'm mute
wallpaper, whispering
just to catch

my breath.

Process notes

Peter writes: Colette Jonopulos is my best friend in the whole world. What's odd about that is I've never met her. I came into contact with Colette when I submitted work to Tiger's Eye (which she co-edits) in Spring of 2007. She was kind and wise and funny, so I kept writing her back and never stopped.

I came to poetry seriously at about the end of 2003. Well, that's when I started publishing. I don't think I was very good until about 2007. Anyway, Colette was born writing poetry and has attended and ran many workshops and seminars. She's a true student of the craft. So, I often read her my work over the phone and she points out the one or two lines that are utterly ridiculous. Gently, of course.

So it was natural that I came to her with "in the trade," one of my truest "character" poems to date. It's from the point of view of a lonely prostitute and since I'm not even a woman, I thought maybe Colette could add some reality to the piece. And she did. I won't tell you which lines were hers but if you love one in particular — it's probably hers.

Lost in Waukesha

Karla Huston and Cathryn Cofell

Like a flock of confused birds,
Thigh finds herself running head
long into the dark, the sky a shawl
of witches, caught in this spell
of minutes repeating, corners
without edges or names,
street lights blown out, the wind
like an unnamed thought.
Even the bright seeds of stars
are planted deep tonight;
this is how it feels to be planted
deep, buried alive.
The path once seemed so clear
the shuffle of her feet, shift of hip
clutch   brake   shift   clutch
to get a grip, to remember this
is only a temporary loss in the suburbs,
this is not the detour of her life.

Process notes

This poem was inspired literally by getting lost in Waukesha, Wisconsin, a city with which we
were unfamiliar. Trying to drive home after a late-night poetry reading, we were hopelessly turned
around and not for the first time. One of us made a joke about writing a poem in which our Thigh
character was also lost, when we arrived home (finally), one of us took up the charge by writing the
first couple of lines. Since we'd often used Exquisite Corpse to collaborate, we wrote two lines each
back and forth by email (with the first line xxx'd out) until we agreed upon a line count and an ending. This one came out with few changes — pretty amazing!

For general notes on their collaborative process, see Miracle Fish, pg. 28

bingo dye calligraphy grid

Andrew Topel and Jim Leftwich

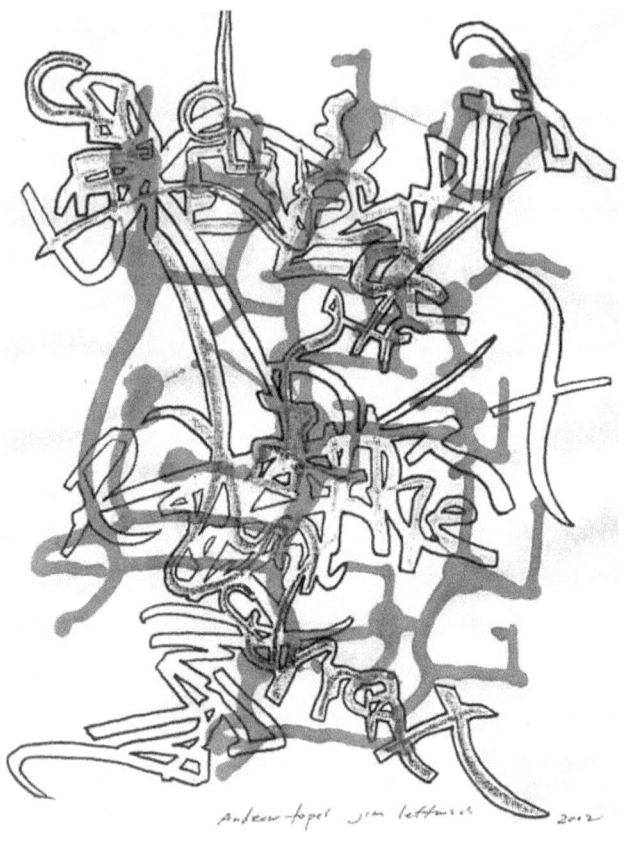

Process notes

Andrew writes: Collaboration is an important, vital part of creating for me. Both art and writing are acts of creation usually done in isolation. It can be intimidating to stare at a blank canvas or an empty sheet of paper, seeing nothing but white space. Collaboration allows one to break free from the isolation and generate new ideas. Through collaborative work, the artistic act becomes a process of give-and-take, a dialogue opening up between two or more people, and brings a tremendous amount of heat and surprise to the creative process. It can lead one down new and unexplored neural pathways. I highly recommend that everyone share his/her vision with another/others, and let another's vision seep into their minds, intertwining and super-congealing brain-cells, then create together and shield your eyes from the potential explosion.

Jim writes:
1 - consensus reality is always collaborative
2 - the construction of meaning is always collaborative
3 - subjectivity is always collaborative

---

blood_alley://interstital_syn.tax

Dethe Elza and Daniela Elza

alleys(have no fixed addresses):
no front door stoops;

shortcuts coding the city
with their pragmatic and dirty

/* kind of beauty. an apothem's
relentless straightedge */

functions() of a hyperbolic map
where roads only turn right;

<the> alley fails a pi[d]geon-faced dealer
his bicycle navigating </crowds>

whoDwellBehind theNormals in
life. thisMetaspace of precariousCables;

dumpsters_and_bugs   crashing

among-the-crows, the-circuits
of old-benches,   where travellers
chalk their-secret-language

(on (the (underbelly (of) the) city) — here)

a thousand: kilometers of: short cuts
threading the: longest path: through

defeatingspaces

to {the | pharmacy} with {no | pain} killers

Dethe writes: Hearing Daniela every day for the past few weeks talking about one collaboration or another, it just seemed natural to try one together. I sent her a poem about the alleys of Vancouver.

Daniela writes: The alley topic sat dormant in my head for a few days. One night we brainstormed around alleys: these shortcuts, like in coding, and suddenly there was an explosion of ideas. Especially after the lights went out. To the point that we wrote notes under the light of a cellphone, thinking that was it. We laugh now, why we did not turn the light on.

Dethe: I have often wondered how to put computers and technology into poetry. Poetry has had a big influence on how I write code, but the influence hasn't gone the other way very much. The sparking of these ideas helped to bring the two together.

Daniela: I could not go to sleep. I got up and wrote trying to give shape to what had just happened. It was 2am when I finally settled down. I sent that to Dethe the next day.

Dethe: When I went through it, each line triggered new ideas. Under each line I wrote the line it inspired: a re-working of Daniela's line, and sometimes a more drastic change. The result was like taking the poem through a looking-glass, basically the same, but also entirely different. I thought it was really shaping up.

Daniela: When I got his email, I was shocked. It felt like he did not keep a lot of the phrasing. I felt like I introduced stress in the process by commenting on that. But when I looked at it the next day, I realized what he was doing. He was riffing off, tightening up, taking out what he did not want. I rewrote the poem using my lines and his lines.

Dethe: With a couple of very small changes, I was happy with it. At this point, the poem felt done to me. There was one word that was misspelled ("pidgeon") and I wanted to keep it because we were using a pigeon both as imagery and as metaphor (alley denizens), while we were also playing with language, especially the simplified pidgin language of computers. I resolved this by putting the "d" in square brackets, then mentioned that it made it look kind of like code.

Daniela: At this point I wanted it to look more like code, and asked Dethe to go further, to introduce different aspects of coding.

Dethe: The result isn't really code, but it carries the feel of various programming languages. A different programming language or construct is reflected in pretty much every stanza. Trying to work those constructs in without destroying or distracting overly from the poem was a challenge. I still don't know if it was successful or if we pushed it too far.

Puebla de los ángeles

Arturo Lomas Garza, Robert Skiles, and Katherine Durham Oldmixon

On the zócalo in Puebla, *la ciudad de los ángeles*,
flocks of shiny balloons rise and fall and rise
again with the coruscating spray of water
spouted from the mouths of fountain
fish misting birds who flutter

above human voices

peddlers, priests, tourists folding
maps, laughing children playing chase,
rumble of taxis, buses, cars, clink of glasses in
sidewalk cafes, scrape of chairs as the band begins
the danzón, hum of horns, scuff of cellos and violins,

lyrical silence of pigeon wings.

(This is the text of a multimedia video which can be viewed on the website. -Eds.)

Process notes

Robert Skiles and Arturo ("Turo") Lomas Garza have been friends and collaborators for almost thirty-three years, together performing Robert's musical compositions for recordings and live concerts. Poet and photographer Katherine Durham Oldmixon and Turo have also worked together and supported one another on many artistic projects. So it's no surprise that Turo, the editor of this project, is the nexus of the collaboration.

When we launched this project, we agreed that we wanted Robert's music to be central, but we began with Katherine's poem "Puebla de los ángeles" as a basis for the idea. Robert had read the poem before and expressed an appreciation for its sounds and images. We didn't want the poem to become lyrics accompanied by music, but the music to be its own interpretation and representation of the idea, and the poem and images to complement. So Robert wrote and recorded his piano solo, "Puebla de los ángeles," and Turo selected and edited Katherine's photographs of Puebla, Mexico to create the visual media, integrating the lines of the poem as he heard them and saw them in the song.

Why No One Saw It Coming

Susan Elbe and Ron Czerwien

The accelerating street was wet light
and we were, impossibly, on ledges
                    talking down the suicides,

disarming the shooters on their way to school,
            the night's echolocation
                        giving way to

the heart's,
            and though *a signal is not an answer*

sometimes even a glimpse of the Divine Yes
is enough,
            the quick of it
                        almost mocking

            a life laboring to break
bewilderment's code.

What if we took in the street preacher?
Silenced the fortune teller?
                        Laid off
each sure thing?

Maybe all we need to remember is how
            to call the sun up
                        or pin down the moon.

Maybe we're merely steps
                    away from nowhere.

Process notes

The process began one evening while we were browsing the fiction display at our local Borders Bookstore. One of us suggested that some of the book titles might make good titles for collaborative poems. Ron chose the title from that list and also submitted the first line. We then composed the poem strictly via e-mail. Early on Ron asked if we should offer edits during the process, but Susan felt we'd lose the energy of the exchange. So we simply continued to alternate lines. The varying line lengths and freer use of white space were Susan's ideas. Ron followed her lead. Susan's poems are replete with words that are surprising but never arbitrary. Ron offers as a good example of this her use of "echolocation." Ron's post-modern leanings stretched Susan's approach.

Our biggest stumbling block was sticking with it. Our busy lives and other work intruded, and we constantly had to prod each other to come back to the collaboration. There were long periods when both of us struggled to come up with the right line, one that would not only carry forward what came before but also lead towards a felt, though always unknown, conclusion. The poem even includes a line Ron appropriated from a poem by Rae Armantrout, who he was reading at the time of the collaboration. Oddly enough, all of our lines survived editing! We each thought very carefully about what psychic gift we were sending the other person. Susan loved anticipating what the next line from Ron would be. Both of us think it's important to collaborate with someone whose work and sensibility you enjoy and respect, but having different styles makes it more interesting. We hope to do more together in the future.

White: A Ghazal

Scott Wiggerman and Andrea L. Watson

An alabaster moon — sere and chaste as salt.
Loneliness: an imagined lake, sad-faced as salt.

A thin refrain settles like ashes on flesh.
Breath like smoke, thick as a paste of salt.

Nest of snakes on desert grains, a dry-boned season.
Wind veils the way, gusts of white laced with salt.

O pray for women of the pearl tattoo!
Such yearning to feel disgraced with salt.

Truth is oracle and mirage, is it not?
An infidel is buried to his waist in salt.

Caravans sense roads like soles to nowhere —
All the ancient shrines defaced by salt.

Oblivion asks the nomad only this to live:
What would you give to taste such salt?

Process notes

Scott: After reading qarrtsiluni's call for submissions for a "Mutating the Signature" issue, I knew I wanted to try writing collaboratively, something I'd never done before or even thought of doing. I immediately contacted Andrea Watson — my first choice in a "partner" — to see if she might be interested, as I knew her work to be inventive, lovely, and similar to my own in imagery and style.

Andrea: I was delighted when Scott Wiggerman contacted me about collaborating on this poetry project. I had admired his writing for years and was happy to have made his acquaintance in a workshop at the Taos Summer Writers Conference several years ago. Then we performed with other artists and poets at an ekphrastic event, Interwoven Illuminations, at the historic Rane Gallery, in Taos, New Mexico last year. I respected his knowledge of poetic technique and his approach to poetry. This collaboration was meant to be!

The only problem — a matter of miles! 735.70 to be precise. And so, email became our modus operandi.

Scott: And so began a series of thirty-plus emails in less than a month! I did not see distance as a problem; in fact, I saw it as an opportunity to collaborate with someone whom I couldn't see on a day-to-day basis. The miles quickly became immaterial.

Andrea: I had collaborated with two women writers on a novel but had never written poetry with another person. Ever. And Scott was suggesting one of the poems be a sonnet! Oh boy! We would each write a line, back and forth, of the quatrains, but we would be free to change a word or two of the other person's line if we wished. Soon, the sonnet took shape — a crow, powerful, menacing, ebony. Black became a central motif of the evolving Shakespearean sonnet.

Thus, the color white begged to be the other motif. We chose the ghazal, a form with which I have been comfortable, and the white motif lent itself to a desert landscape. We chose to write a couplet apiece, the ghazal flowing and telling us what it wanted. We dialogued back and forth, added details, subtracted conflicting imagery, kept refining as we went along. We kept the ghazal to fourteen lines, based on an innovative ghazal/sonnet we had seen by poet Sandra Dolin.

Scott: Even in our choice of poetic forms (not that they were required), we took a collaborative approach. I had initially suggested we write two formal sonnets and that we each write the first line to one, then alternate lines after that. This is in fact how we approached the "black" sonnet. But Andrea suggested we make the second poem a ghazal, or more precisely a ghazal/sonnet, basically a ghazal of fourteen lines, and she provided the opening couplet, which we agreed would be focused on the color white.

We worked simultaneously on both the sonnet and the ghazal (something new for me, as I usually work on only one poem at a time), adding lines day after day — and offering suggestions for preceding lines, phrases, and/or words. In our back-and-forth banter, we joked about sending "draft 11 million"! At one point, I described the daily revision to Andrea as "hyper-critiquing."

Andrea: And we were diligent, nay crazy, in our approach. We wrote every day, no matter what, and made sure to touch base as the poems came to life. The holidays were on the horizon — with guests, travels, too much food, not enough wine — but we continued to email until Christmas was upon us. By then, the two poems — the two forms — had matured, and so we let the work sit. I tinkered on the airplane. Scott looked at the poems amidst a house of visitors. It would be wise to let the poems breathe....

Scott: And to let ourselves breathe too!

Andrea: Later, we removed a word of two from the ghazal that conflicted with white. We kept reworking the last couplet of the sonnet. It needed to be powerful but not overpower the poem.

Scott: Though we let the drafts of the two poems "breathe" over the holidays, we already had spent quite a bit of time revising and fine-tuning them. We constantly checked with each other to see what the other thought about any changes, being respectful but blunt. Honesty was something we both required and cherished.

Andrea: It is important to note that while poets have different styles, different views of metaphor or imagery, poets represent what is so hopeful about the Humanities: people collaborating together on a project such as this; people conversing with one another to make something fine; people celebrating the wonder-work of being human in the twenty-first century. And poetry is the golden thread that binds us all together.

Scott: Our "mutating" was so rewarding that we've both thought of continuing the process throughout 2009 (and beyond?). Someday you may see a whole chapbook of Watson/Wiggerman poems! Thank you, qarrtsiluni, for sparking this creativity!

American Way

Andy Anderson; Music by Andy and Ryan Hoke, Wild Goose Creative

Somewhere on the prairie,
A bison is learning to use an axe.
He is not good at it.
He has no opposable thumbs,
So he can't really swing the axe with much
Accuracy. Plus he keeps on trying to eat the handle,
It is made of wood, and for some reason
Looks delicious to the bison, even though
Most bison eat grass. After being distracted
By the delicious looking handle for the
Umpteenth time, the bison finally manages
To get a good clean swing in.
The trick is putting the handle in
The mouth, not for eating but for holding,
And whipping the head around.
Now that the bison has learned
To use the axe, he realizes
With the little brainpower
That he possesses, that there is nothing
To cut down on the prairie.
The bison has finally learned the American way:
Learning a skill that has no practical application.
He might has well have learned to
Juggle chainsaws.

Process notes

Last Spring we had the idea to work together collaboratively on some poetry. We'd been reading each others work for a while but wanted a project we could work on together. We began sharing poems back and forth like a conversation, letting the last poem sent by one serve as a starting place for the next poem written by the other. To raise the stakes we gave each other a 72-hour time frame to be inspired, write something new, and respond.

It was interesting because our styles were very different at the outset — one of us tends toward the more absurd and delineated (Andy) while the other works more with the idea of straightforward storytelling and rhythmic language (Ryan). The four poems that will appear in qarrtsiluni comprise a section from the beginning of the process, where we were still figuring out how to respond to one another and very much using the styles we were used to. However, over time we began to learn how to explore each other's styles and found our methods changing in response to one another, slowly drawing out previously unexplored nuances, themes, and styles.

Life Lessons

Andy Anderson; Music by Andy and Ryan Hoke, Wild Goose Creative

My tiny fist disappeared
into the horse's nostril.
Before I knew what I was doing
I had plunged my hand wrist
deep into that soft round,
perfectly fist shaped opening.

The horse snorted
and glanced at me
as if to say "The hell was that?"
and Chip, the Toronto zoo horse trainer extraordinaire
said something like "uh...whoa..easy there little buddy."

Six year old violates horse nostril on first trip to Canada.

Two days previous my family had
sling shotted over the boarder
and into the Ontario wilderness
straight stretches of flat road.
In our pockets
my sister and I clutching the Canadian quarters
my father had gifted us.

American dreaming,
kindergarten king of the back seat,
my sister and I slept on a dusty mattress
in the back of our brown station wagon.

Next, since the pieces we write are meant to be performed, we decided to choose several poems and add some original beats and music. This was an entirely new collaborative process for us as well — jointly discussing and choosing which tempos and rhythms worked best, creating new music as needed (Andy) and getting a crash course on music software (Ryan).

This collaboration is ongoing and has been a great source of creative inspiration and artistic accountability, giving us the opportunity to generate a good chunk of new work but also to be open to being influenced and changed by each other.

The same brown station wagon
that every nuclear family from 1979-82
seemed to have been issued.
Like it was a government sponsored program,
an exercise in hegemony,
for the families of our great nation to all own
the same awkwardly geared , wood veneered, chocolate seared
elephantine, gas greedy shrine
chunk of metal
and suburban optimism.

100 degree heat
we sweated in the morning sleep
and trundled to the Toronto zoo.
I remember there were foot prints
painted on the pavement indicating
"Walk here. Don't veer off to the left.
There are lions to the left and you will be eaten.
Stick to the footprints."

Days end, one horse nostril later,
100 degree heat reduced to 85,
tightly squeezed in the zoo tram transport
main entrance to battle scarred car,
my father taught me about the middle finger
how I shouldn't single it out,
shouldn't press it against the widow
innocently greeting shocked Canadians.

I was only enjoying the finger feeling
of the rub haltingly squealing on the hot pane
the sound of it squeaking, creaking
against the smooth glass.
But I'm sure in that moment
I looked like just another American.

Already my time abroad
was teaching me valuable life lessons
maturing innocence and forever changing
the way I looked at middle fingers
a secret dirty word hidden inside each one.

Him or Me

Andy Anderson; Music by Andy and Ryan Hoke, Wild Goose Creative

I realize now that it was a big mistake
to purchase a Zebra sight unseen.
More caution was necessary,
and I'd been foolish to make such
a large transaction on the internet
with a company that I didn't even know.
The animal was delivered in a large crate
that could only be opened with a crowbar,
giving the delivery vehicle plenty of time
to get away, as I didn't have a crowbar
handy at the time of the delivery.
When I finally got the crate open after
a half hour of banging and swearing,
I immediately realized that the so-called
"zebra" was in fact a horse that had been
painted to look like a zebra.
Poorly painted, I might add,
as there was paint slopped everywhere,
some of which wasn't even completely dry.
Not that it wasn't a very nice horse,
probably a thoroughbred from the
look of him. Worth more than I had
paid perhaps, but I didn't want a horse,
I wanted a Zebra. That was what I
had ordered. Referring to the internet
receipt, I called the customer service number
and instead of unhelpful call center workers
got an adult chat hotline. Surprisingly,
they were of no help either, even after I explained
the whole situation to them.
Disappointed, I went back outside
and found the horse eating all of my flowers.
He'd already made a huge mess in my driveway
and kicked in the driver's side window of
my car. He had quite a temper, which was
understandable because he was likely upset
about having been painted to look like a zebra,
when he was obviously a horse.
We'd both been deceived, that was for sure,
although I still don't know who was worse off
for it, him or me.

326 Miles North

Ryan Hoke; music by Ryan and Andy Anderson, Wild Goose Creative

He washes dishes downtown
and I can see him drown
the forks and spoons
spraying dinner plates
spinning steam like cocoons.

His 17 year old frame
tight knit sinew speaks to muscle
bears the weight of the world's hustle
built for highs school hallways
literal lightning of broad shoulders
force summer sun comparisons always
shirtless shinings as he subtlety flexes his
brotherly bravado
testing, chest to chest.

I love him.
I love him.
I love him.

Esau demanding that Jacob
put to rest the grudges of youth
snapping the fraternal yards stick
hands soft but quick
refusing to notch my claim against the wall
of family history.

9 years.
9 years between birth and new birth.
He watched as I two stepped first
waiting like shovel
poised over new earth
mitigated mirth
so he too
could shirk the lazy burden of youth
tucked deep into rural reckonings of
blueberry farms, convenience stores
and suburban family dysfunction.

I took flight
for academic ease at seventeen leaving
the day to day of sibling laughter
my eyes already tired from
the weight and heat of home
but he waited
like a crepe paper balloon
hollowed out as elastic dreams
popped and shriveled

spun and swiveled
boyishly battled with unraveled seams.

He waited.
Waited.
Waited.

Anticipated
until adolescent hurt
simmered to righteous anger
at the people, places and things
that had made fraudulent claims
about how sons should be raised.

And now
I wait as he waits
watching as taciturn toes
tap and turn towards the tide
the inevitable gravitational pull
towards the feather strong feel of
light and orbiting inertia
standing on the edge of precipices
so ordinary and so dangerous they
shimmer like electrified copper pennies.

I wait as he waits
for some dark night
when adult agility will knock at his
window
calling to war
swift strings of real romance and
hands that are ready to heal.

But now
he leans against a full sink
waits without knowing he's waiting
co-creating, washing dishes downtown
I can see him drown
the forks and spoons
spraying fate in the face
and spinning steam like cocoons.

Process notes
Andy was especially involved on "326 Miles
North" in creating the entire guitar line
underneath. (For additional process notes, see
page 72.)

Reflective Borders

Dorothee Lang and Steve Wing

Process notes

Dorothee: Collaboration is the central element of these months: since a good while, I am part of the group writing project 2028, which connects 7 authors from different continents. Steve is also part of this group, and with both of us being contributors to qarrtsiluni, the idea of working together on a submission seemed like an interesting challenge. It was good timing, too: as 2028 is mainly about revisions right now, the 'merged signature' theme brought us back to the try-and-explore phase of a collaboration.

Steve: After initially working with mixed media, we decided to work purely with images. We each suggested themes with many possible interpretations, settling on 'reflective' and 'borders.' We each emailed the other some images, then worked with the other's photos and our own, cropping and combining them to create a collaborative collage. These flew back and forth across the Atlantic as we revised and worked toward a finished version.

Dorothee: That's how "Reflective Borders" came together. In fact, it's a double merger - a merging of the two photo themes: 'reflective' and 'borders', and the combining of digitally rendered photos into a black/white collage.

Steve: Working with Doro's photos was interesting, knowing that each represents not just a view from another continent, but also something she experienced. It was like a secret hidden in the photo. And of course, with my images, I know some of its secrets. Like in Reflective Borders, one of these places no longer exists.

Dorothee: The process had the feeling of an adventure, a journey, and I think this is true also of the finished work.

We Wrote a Letter to Jesus and He Told Us To Buy a New Car

Arlene Ang and Valerie Fox

There were sinister red marks on the dog where its hair came off

I had just moved back to the city after having been away for three years at school

It was around the same time I went out on a blind date with someone and dropped my keys under the bar at the Villa de Roma

Although I had no money I had several typewriters

In our childhood, we were all victims of DDT

I kept wiping my mouth on parts of the table napkin that I hadn't soiled with my lipstick

The more I learned about my driving from rude strangers, the more I understood extinction

It seemed like everyone back then was making a film using one of those toy video cameras Fisher Price had come out with

On the ground, an egg sandwich absorbed the rain and disintegrated down the gutter

The sound of the CAT scan was just gaining prominence, getting louder and louder with each passing season

Poor as I was, I had friends with less

The museum was free on Sundays but I had to buy them coffee and once, a tuna melt

Since that day at the beach my digestive tract began to exist outside of my body

In the back of our heads somewhere — voices of our great-grandparents speaking in German, comfortable in their lonesome canal-town

The new car turned out to be a rainy-blue '64 Buick Skylark with taped-on plastic material for the rear view mirror instead of glass

The way I'm lighting all these candles to save electricity makes me a real fire hazard

A lot of pretending goes into the appearance of water and electricity

For larks, we used to pretend we were courtiers, and our dog was of the 5th rank

I documented many aspects of our lives, but not our dog's

Fifteen years later I remember the look of the crowd but not what the speaker said

Once I start listing them I can remember hundreds of these crowds

That must mean something

I see plenty of famous people (celebrities) around town but I forget them within seconds

Dear Me, I used to start a lot of letters that way

One conversation stands out, on a beach in Atlantic City

We had nicknames for everyone both consequential and inconsequential

I got a bit of advice from sisterly types about what to do about my name at the neighborhood bar

We heard people spray graffiti on the side of our house and it wasn't even that late

Homes were sinking too, there were sinkholes

The whole time everything was happening I kept trying to find words to describe our own small, austere circumstance

Dogs woke us up early each and every day

It was alright to waste our time as long as we could choose how to waste it

For process notes, see "In retrospect, 1984 made a fine sausage," pg. 40.

Similarities

Peter Cherches and Holly Anderson

The fetchingly lithe and charmingly disheveled Ms. Tetley-Pringle was well into the third hour of her daily asanas when truth called down to her like a thunderclap:

A clock has a floor and a ceiling and four walls. A clock also has a window. Some, but not all, clocks have doors.

A telephone, not unlike a clock, has four walls, a floor and a ceiling. All telephones also have doors. Some, but not all, telephones have windows.

She forgot her 13th or 14th Downward Facing Dog of the day and hit the sticky mat belly first. In considerable pain she considered her prosthetic limb. She preferred the old-fashioned wooden sort to the lighter and infinitely more wieldy synthetic variety, believing this choice gave her practice a better chance of finally attaining true liberation.

Ms. Tetley-Pringle tried again to empty her mind but found herself considering the startling similarities among disparate objects such as prosthetic limbs, bowls of breakfast cereal, and the books of the Old Testament. She now understood with utter clarity that all have four walls, windows, a floor and a ceiling. Each also has a door. And one day one of these doors will open into a post office and a young man with snow on his shoulders will rush up to a clerk, with an urgency he never knew he was capable of and shout, "My grandmother has broken her hip. You must go to her at once!"

For process notes, see "Found Photo," pg. 23.

the lid's off, the secret's out

Andrew Topel and Spencer Selby

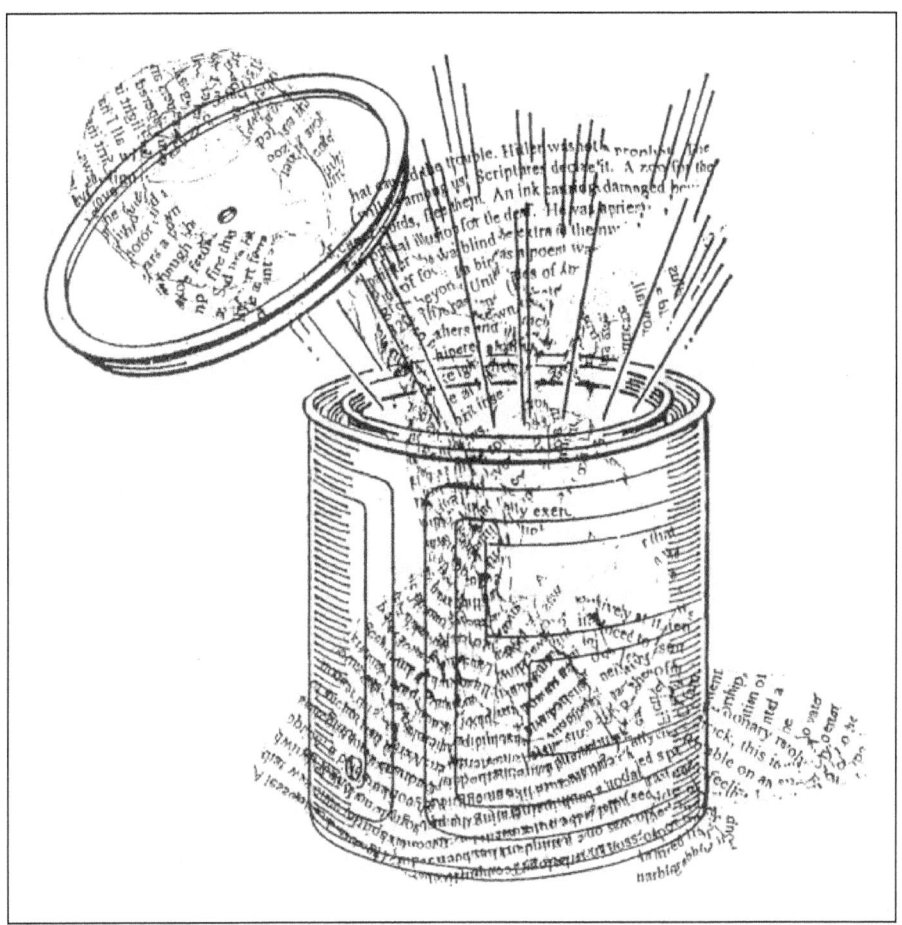

Jaw Plants

John M. Bennett and Stacey Allam

Ah jaw ah lamp ah dent
ah plates of braided spaghetti
tongued elbow gleaming
slick spit nestled on the gown you
folded in the shower
that slipped guppies
down its crease
and quipped like skull
reflected off the floor
mobility of all those
wind blown banners
hopping on the porches
and eating up all the plants

Process notes

John told us that he and Stacey use the postal service for their collaborations, sending a piece back
and forth, each adding usually one line at a time until they both feel it's done.

Zuihitsu: Botanical Traces

Pamela Hart and Steve Rago

Image by Steve Rago

Herbarium

Perfection wounds the single
leafed beauty pressing
against glass to blot
out a patch of grey light
splintering winter's work,
its chill, its ice. We peer
through a window to sheen
of jungle bright, study leaf
rib and spine, find worn
symmetry in petiole and blade.
Is this how memory
is found, some unclaimed
thing, a trace of botany
blooming at the vanishing point?

by Pamela Hart

Process notes

We started with a strategy, but to paraphrase John Lennon, art is what happens when you get
busy making other plans. Our idea had been to wander around the New York Botanical Garden,

independently and together, with camera and notepad, to dig for content. The Enid A. Haupt Conservatory and the 250-acre-garden grounds, seemed, especially in winter, like good locations for capturing germination and mutation. We had planned to spend time looking, photographing and writing on our own. Then we'd find a particular "thing" that called to us and share that beloved treasure (plant, sculpture, architecture, whatever) with the other. Once material was generated, studio work would proceed.

The best-laid plans went awry at the ticket counter when we learned we wouldn't be able to visit the Conservatory (the place with all the cool plants) due to a holiday show. So we walked around the grounds. Frustrated by the lack of access, we peered from the outside into the beautiful hothouse, looking at the weird and wild plant life that pushed at the paneled glass.

This decision proved fruitful. From the outside looking in, Steve found and photographed leaves and reflections. Pam was intrigued by the way exotic plants seemed to clamor for escape, and by the layering of cityscape and Edenic scenery. Our stumbling block had become a platform for collaboration.

Later, in putting together image and text, both of us let go of brainstorming notions on arrangement to let the words and photographs collide and combine as we played with page layout, stanza and line breaks and even with the title. The Japanese notion of zuihitsu seemed a final important element. Ultimately, the piece — text and image — excerpted here exists as a series of interconnected essays, fragmented and then woven together on the page. These are our contemplations on the rather unnatural environment we discovered one winter afternoon, which turned out to be, quoting from poet Robert Duncan, a place of "first permission, everlasting omen of what is."

Two Girls Decorating a Cat by Candlelight

Elisa Gabbert and Kathleen Rooney

The cat decelerates at the sight of the negligee,
but negligibly, she's a feisty little thing. It's like
she knows the difference between cheap & brilliant,
& costume jewels are for the proverbial birds
who chirp in the rafters, heavy on the reverb.
Dragging her ribbons she darts to the window —
the sweet release of death, to the feline,
is a self-indulgent wish. She purrs at the snow
& her fur is windblown. Do the girls
interpret her shivers as fear or something
fancier? Dancing animals populate
their dreams. It is almost dreamtime,
so say the clock's glockenspiels.
Say goodnight to the haloed room.

Process notes

"Two Girls Decorating a Cat by Candlelight" is an ekphrastic poem based on the painting by
Joseph Wright of Derby.

For more notes on the authors' collaborative process, see "Rasterization," pg. 60.

Split Personality

Karla Huston and Cathryn Cofell

I'm a swift walker
a queen bed rocker
a girdle stalker
a spider smacker
a monkey pile
a trip down that girl's aisle,
a stay at home mom-o-phile.
Shape shifter, beauty grifter,
sexual drifter
watch me jiggle and whistle,
I'm built like a missile.
I'm waiting for you, tucked in lush grass.

Or maybe I'm a little slimmer
a moon-y glimmer, a blinking
swimmer in an old fish eye.
The one you wish for,
the one you'd hiss for, so
pack this cellulite
in your momma's sigh.
I'm nearly darling, a timeless
starling, a little more care–
less than free.
So bring us the hum,
a symphony of drums, the rumble
of a good epiphany.

Process notes

Cathryn wrote the first stanza after a conversation about a persona we'd created for our collaborative work, some jokes about funny poems the persona would write if she had the chance. Since the persona is a character called "Thigh," it made sense that we imagined her with a twin, one she didn't always get along with, one who wasn't exactly the same. After Cathryn wrote the first stanza, Karla responded with the other "leg" of the story.

Coup d'État

Greta Aart and Sally Molini

The teacher refuses to open the door,
    at odds with her profession.

Of course you know why. You answered
her questions with three
blank pages — no need to be verbal,
her omniscient nerve sees all. You write
in transparent ink.

The class turns rowdy. Roars and whistles.
You feel happy but can't shake some lurking
disappointment. So you honk from your nickel-plated
seat like a clown.

The teacher repeats her sentence,
    inconsiderate of your obvious
innocence.

You swear to tell the truth — instead, a last punch
to the teacher's glasses.
They slide off
the cliff of her nose. A spectacle, like every word
from her lips
    passing down the highway
of your hyperbolic mind.

Stand outside and pull your ears!

So you tilt your head and see
the inverse sky.
Windows tipped like wings, clouds
look so soluable.
When you rub your eyes, the clouds
fall as tears. Swallow
them — they taste like salt and light.

For process notes, see "Vanishing Biography," pg. 11.

liquid

John Cese (A.K.A. Andrew Topel) and Paul Brandt

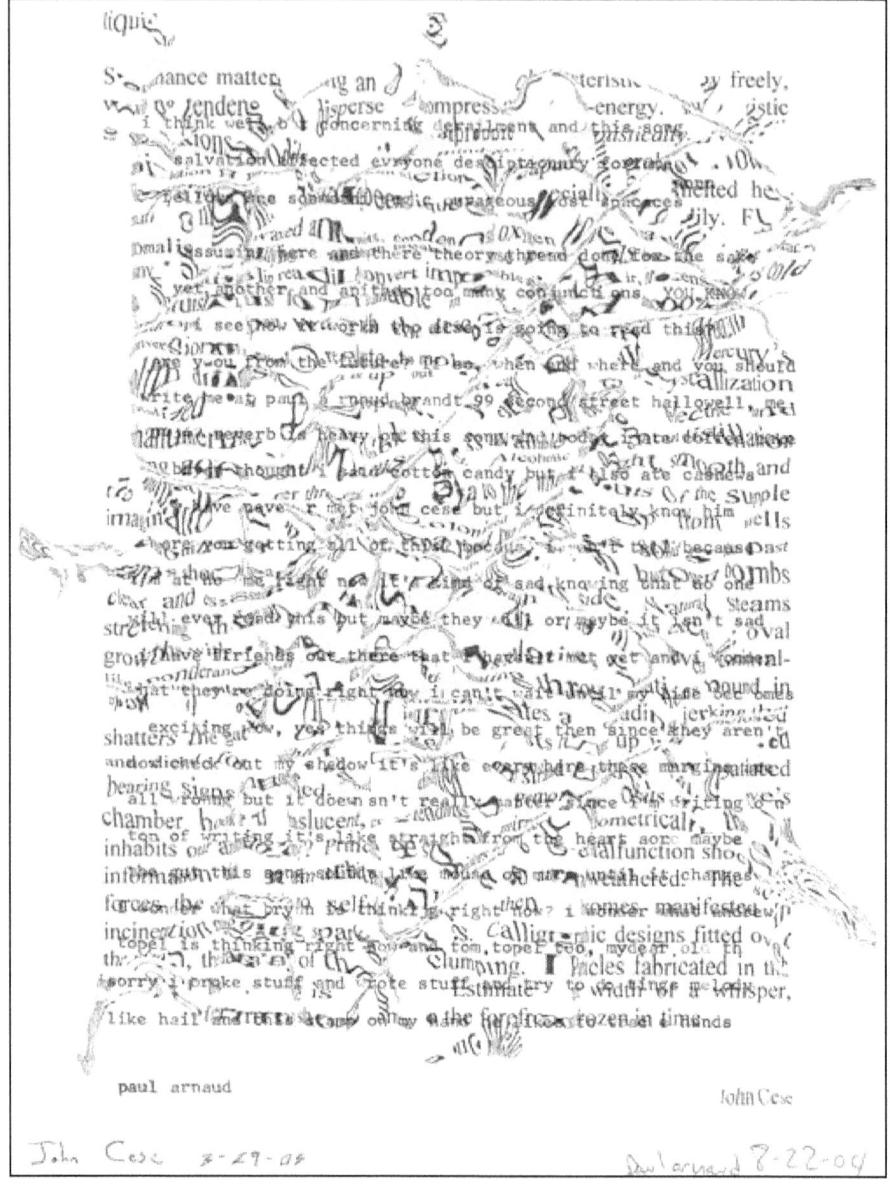

Monster: a Glottochronology

Thomas Cook and Tyler Flynn Dorholt

Dear River,

> *I imagine you apologize for the fish.*
> *My wooden stomach: hook the fins as want stiffens.*
> *I hear the mud tremble & back up slow unto.*

This side of the moon can only offer one course. Did anyone truly give the idea it was made of cheese a chance? Pause. Maybe we should organize ourselves around such beliefs again, give us a sense nature is still mysterious beyond the flashbulbs, let us crack a bit stepping into the river. Let me run my finger over those rocks. I'll split it with you. You've grown another seed in your window & you expect the best. Fine. It is here I put my foot down. What hope do you have of relocating the sun? For a moment, try feeding your bones, bones. Let's take the foot out for a spin. It was just down the way they planted all those trees, wouldn't it be nice to see. At the heart of great exposures, something minute tarrying film. Carry that around in your head. I give other oil. In our glottal dreams, we always arrive the fine substance. This glass is tricky. Flush in a pinch around the edges. Take the mongrel out. Hope a call comes. I think I've heard that one in an instant. Better backtrack & jackal norms will appear, absolving us of this rush for something keening. I remember lying in the sail.

Dear Bridge,

> *I imagine your thoughts about the moon being on.*
> *My bones fed: the astral oils are changed as trees sleep.*
> *I fondle like a plant the new airs with my scent.*

And how is it that you want us to call at this as home? Only seminal apertures, or making your kiss. The top five most emotional albums of your life hint at some religion & stake at yacht forebodings. Not necessarily owning real property are we? Your toes in your fingers, would you consider a grounding, or in getting to carry patterns over-warm the one skin? How uncomfortable is this theatre? — & you wanted to call in early for the other seat: piffle. Here I hear most about saying something over the streams — it is that rock just out of focus that I sat on naked & made geyser. There could have been other consumptions, but you tent-ended viscosity. Laundry in the middle of the night, cleaning up the rugs they footed while mouth-washing: penultimate. Secondly, when has the shade drawn down on lust? Hand of God gnaws on dog-leg, seeks out the filaments of rue. At the unmoving patch in the marina, blessings waver, blessings splash, and I feel cowgirls with binoculars upon this, I feel rearrival in the strongest stage of snow set on by sun, its salvaging, its sniff, my chance, your sign, is raring to go & get back to fitting in.

* * *

Dear River,

> *I am returning these pebbles for the uprise.*
> *My going through: a small line fixates on current.*
> *I am a good look for passing planes & sculptures.*

The torpors loomed, to recount the spread of the maladroit check off the shoe lather, laces unhinged: occlude the incursion of the decrepitude charmer; oft & bungled the coin purse. Our dearth is to heft because baseborn we traverse the aftertaste of phone calls with lady-lady. Because I offer fins I'm ichthyic? I am fully-grown & functioning, use one belt for the holler, & strove once to bundle me shingles. It took the dukes & a farming crowd: they left in unexpected hook: scale. The secret I've been keeping for years is out: jet out the jug & lo & be & hold for you're a mover: wed: you roof the boom, foam up the vase & stem out toward diligence. They offer such settlement it stirs> I will offer my ex composure< in the snap I didn't perfect there sits hindrance, from other depths, at its best: thumb: in the earliest embryo I moon-hung atop the solar asymmetries of the stomach: rumbled: knew not the intestinal focus as it stood with facts. Since the recourse, we've gone off exchange. I want to tell why two bananas: you ought to keep it all as useful as suspenders. Too heavy for the table, the child decries its biscuit as drop-giggle — off the calcification: pacifier, you hold unheard sins, palm little lungs. There are too many cold cuts out in the other room, let's pass pastries & be again the baby. We are bottled in the waxing of the moon.

Dear Bridge,

> *I suspend a frame for the over then nethers.*
> *My weaning: the absence of our good old ducky.*
> *I scent the ascent & take you manually.*

Another magnetized thread takes its place though none of us were around to count the striations. We view the pile of colorful glasses, they will all have merged & we say just what it means to be connected. Yes, I know, of course. Flambeaux, resistance to implicit-ness, epistemic like crystals, caissons, stung by myths of powder like a spike through a clock — whoosh — only a moment ago misled, a candidate, now you flounder in some-one else's subjective account of the history that interpolates you. I would guess you have not used the same pitcher for reconstitute of milk as for fresh. We line up on the coast & skip stones together across the ocean surface. Smoke billows up from strategic points within the walls of the city. Tintinnabulations deliver one back, bedizened, transmittance only the essential architecture. Patch up speaking in tongues with thick mouth vapor. The sun fickles its heat, actually & persuades another direction for melt & to live out one's life on the borders of a very thin puddle. New understandings in the voice, in whichever inch it happens. Ribs reveal themselves to be hives digesting lives from a twentieth century horror. A robin goes missing in the field. We trample the summit of the question. We pound the stone. We, everyone crossing the bridge, & shallow sand at the feet. A children to be herd, like a plug, like two pockets return a ghost blank. Similar to the patterns within any place of worship where we find a neutral heart. Cairn, shrugging danger, the dead end for the thoughtless, the try, this whole hovering sidewalk from which plants seek the proper food & the murderer drinks juice. Children are locked-in with their mothers, breaths clipped. Chop of the stalk of celery length-wise. This one will help this other one.

Process notes

A Glottochronology began as a experiment in generative text and is now many divergent experiments that always prove to converge. It has been undertaken almost exclusively through email correspondence over the last 15 months. It all began with this sentence: The state shrunken: if we remove the encasements: which fountain are we at? The project began to metastasize rapidly, gaining speed while the two poets watched short surrealist films together over the phone, incorporating rules applicable to the Oulipo school. One of the projects, swallowed by what the writer's refer to as The Monster, is a book of 125 poems that use all the words in the encyclopedia that begin with the letters g and l. Quite often, the collaboration was done in the same room, in which Thomas and Tyler passed sheets of paper back and forth for long periods of time while Jan Svankmajer films played on the wall. Not a single word or particle has been edited or tinkered with from the original creations. The collaboration has a lifetime roll to it and maintains weekly, if not daily correspondences.

Little Boys and Snips of Donkey Tails

Arlene Ang and Valerie Fox

"It's a children's book launching. Children are necessary. You know that."

Richard hated it when Marie, his marketing agent, spoke to him as if he were a lost-and-found anteater on its way into the eye of a hurricane.

"And pin-the-tail-on-the-donkey always ensures a huge success," she added. It was her way of pointing out a trail of life-saving ants before him.

In the fourteen years they've worked together, Marie never knew Richard's secret: that just because he wrote children's books didn't mean he was actually fond of children. He also wrote a lot about rabbits, and these too he abhorred. After selling four million copies of *The Magical Carpet Bunny in Tahiti*, which he wrote while visiting Gauguin nudes in Paris, he broke into his therapist's office. There he stole most, if not all, of the session tapes with his ramblings and meanderings on bunnies. He still recalls the chill he got when he realized that Dr. Orten actually labeled them "Richard's Rabbits." He'd said (and more): *I keep my allies close but my enemies closer.* And: *I have names for the ways they twitch their ears, how they just lie there, for example, panting in the sun.*

Luckily Dr. Orten didn't notice that someone had stolen the tapes. Richard, after all, still valued their appointments and didn't want to cut her off totally. He knew he could count on her to keep billing even though he cancelled over half of their meetings at the last minute. He needed that time for himself. The paper trail was his name for the arrangement.

Richard's wife, Lorraine, was mildly jealous of Dr. Orten. Richard thought of Lorraine as his wife even though they were no longer married. They'd divorced several years before and had recently reunited-to the displeasure of mutual friends and bankers who preferred Lorraine alone with, perhaps, a bottle of wine. Richard needed a wife like he needed a therapist. He was conscious of this and tried his best to conceal it from both of them. At least Lorraine didn't want kids. Her sprawling home was a perfect ecology for him, in both temperature and in how it faced the sun to the east. He slept and wrote soundly there, without any drug inducement.

"Earth to Richard," chirped Marie through the megaphone.

He could feel himself walking away. Rather rudely. He was past the water cooler and Darcee's desk and half way inside the elevator before he realized what he was doing. He hated it that Marie never ran after him in public. Instead, she used the megaphone which she carried around in her a showy floral hangbag along with pins and plastic balloons.

The only thing Richard was allowed to decide about his book launch was the hour. He made it nine o'clock. As a child, he was never allowed to stay up later than eight. He was counting on the guests to be solely adults, but the adults disappointed him-as always. They came accompanied by their children. Watching them enter, hand in hand or screaming at each other, he felt a sourness sting his mouth.

In Richard's mind a small list, like a contrail, fleeted horizontally in his mind: What Sane People Shouldn't Bring to a Book Party.

Children came up first naturally. Even though they bought or, at least, manipulated their parents to buy his books, he still couldn't think kindly of them. Once, he even received a fan mail from a little girl in Kansas who addressed him as *Dear Santa*. No, there was no liking them at all. Especially after Carmen. He'd been in L.A. for a book appearance five years ago, and was cleaning up Lorraine's place when she called. She mentioned something about being pregnant. It was late in the day, but he still whined, *Do you know what time it is!* He knew he could throw her off every time he made her aware that she never knew what time it was. She had always been quite vulnerable about this, but never cured her low self-esteem by buying a wristwatch. He'd called her crazy and switched off the phone.

Then *jello*. He particularly disliked signing books smudged with strawberry jello. He felt that it took the edge off his pen. Not being allowed to sleep later than eight in the evening can grow a child overnight into a cynic. Green jello was almost as bad. It reminded him of him whenever he thought he could or might have actually gotten anyone with child.

Pin-the-tail-on-the-donkey. This was obvious. Like DNA testing to find out the biological parent. No one ever thought about how the donkey felt. Personally, if he had lost his tail he would've much preferred not to find it, or worse, have it pinned back erroneously on his nose. In his school days, he saw this done every year from his bedroom window. His parents never allowed him to attend any parties because they suspected an alien conspiracy in anything that begins with the letters L-M-N-O-P.

Which brought to his mind *parents*. Somehow it occurred to him that even his parents came generically under the letter P. Aliens. At least, his taught him the meaning of camouflage underwear. They had never warmed up to Lorraine and Marie. Or accepted Dr. Orten as part of the family. Ironically, perhaps, because of their beliefs, they'd have approved of Carmen. When he first met her, she was working in a publishing house. She kept inviting him out for some chocolate pecan pie and finally he relented. He thought it was safe enough. He was even flattered when she wrote herself promiscuous notes under his name and left them in public places-like a phone booth or ice cream parlor. Dear Carmen. She actually thought she could handle his electric knife and still keep her side of his bed.

On the night of the party, Richard got off the elevator on the tenth floor of his building, as usual. It took him but a moment to notice that the party wasn't there at all. Of course, it was across the street at *Le Bec Fin*. He loved their food, but the thought of kids stashing some of it between the pages of his books rather sickened him. The company had gotten a pro to play Chopin or Satie, he was looking forward to that. They'd have some nice champagne, at least. He couldn't think of new ploys to make himself more late, without being too late, so he sighed and pressed Down. When the elevator doors opened there was Marie.

"Thought you'd be here," she laughed. When she grabbed him by the elbow, it was almost friendly. He thought, she might be my friend, this Marie. She might stop bursting balloons with pins to get his attention.

"They'll want to know about your next book, Richard. How is it going?"

Could he tell her? Open up? He was trying to branch out, write about donkeys, even business managers. A story with complications, with a climax-with more than a punchline. Something for a human being for heaven's sake. Stories serious enough to hold ambivalent adult twins (fraternal) and spies in feathered capes. He felt ready for that.

At the same time, he was afraid to know what was going to happen next.

Eventually, Marie pulled him into the party lounge. A crowd of around two hundred was already waiting. And frowns waited heavily on the waiters' faces. The plush oriental carpet had stopped resembling a plush oriental carpet-here and there escargot and roast drippings presented a sort of conceptual art that might've been entitled, "Agoraphobia."

When Marie blindfolded Richard, she left just enough room so he could cock his head and sense the lay of the donkey's rump. Was that Carmen in a Tahitian mouse get-up? Wasn't she transferred in a high-security prison? He never knew whether she was being truthful or sarcastic. The whole two months they were together, she had complained incessantly about where she was, wherever he was, and here she was again.

Sex, he thought, should not be the only subtext for anyone's life, even Carmen's. Or gambling. Or hotels with heated swimming pools and underwater Bach. Lorraine, at least, never suffered such hang-ups, even though now and then she would refuse to wash behind her ears for weeks. Where was she now that he needed to get rid of Carmen?

In the background, he could hear children clap and holler. There was no doubt he'd pin the tail on the damn donkey with aplomb. That wasn't the reason he had all sorts of escape plans weaving in and out of his mind.

Through the slit Marie left for him, he thought he could see the shoulder of a boy. And Carmen's finger was pointing at it.

Process notes

Valerie writes: In "Little Boys and Snips of Donkey Tails," Arlene Ang and I were especially interested in developing the character of Richard, who has been popping up in some way or other in many of the stories we've been writing. We went back and forth with the edits in a highly methodical way. Richard is always on the edge of something, and we think a lot about how obvious we should or should not make this. In some of the stories that feature him we tend to use a lot of description of his physical surroundings, his habitat. This episode explores his mental, voice-filled landscape.

In this interview, Robert Watts discusses with us our ongoing collaborative work: http://drexel.edu/coas/ask/featured-interviews/2008-10-18_valerie-fox-interview_watts.asp

silence: a courtyard

Rob Taylor and Daniela Elza

I shudder   through the bones
of the courtyard

the silence it seeks is a curious   sound

        how speak   a cluster of pines?
    how hold such small   echoes:

words in two voices   a flutter in two
hearts   a finch
I fear to touch   a whisper
behind my ear

under the blooming cherry
this place   a single word
dreamt and   wrapped in dormant
seeds, a slice of black   earth

I clang the gate shut —   the scattered clouds
    look me straight   in the eye
push me about   because they can.

Process Notes

Rob: Our collaboration was preceded by a bit of creative borrowing on both our parts. Having only met once at a local reading, I became enamored with the form Daniela was employing in her work, the triptych: three vertical columns of words that read both horizontally (across the columns, left to right, like a traditional poem) and vertically (down each of the three columns). These triptychs were, in fact, four poems in one, and I was very interested in trying my hand at one (four?). I was especially interested in using blank spaces in the columns to emphasize silences — to see how hollow parts of the poem became when a single word from a single column was removed. I wrote a poem entitled "We speak of silence, not in breath," which focused on the theme of silence and included the sudden interruption of a quiet scene by a bird.

I sent my poem to Daniela, quite unsure if she would either be upset that I was moving in on her form, or dismissive because I didn't really get what the triptych was all about. Instead she was enthusiastic, so much so that when I sent her a note about qarrtsiluni's collaborative writing issue, she quickly responded with a revised version of my poem — and we were off!

Daniela: I sprinkled in nature images, Rob kneaded the emotions in. At first we had a bit of a hiccup. We took too much out. I went back and dragged some of the stuff back in. There were dormant moments between. There were questions: what makes a good poem? I feared about the process at times because I had never done this with someone I practically did not know. I did not want it to fail. All along I cherished the fearless meeting of minds.

Rob: I was nervous about adding to the poem after the initial creative moment. When I edit I am almost always paring away at the poem, but if that's all both people do in a collaborative exercise then pretty soon you have nothing to work with. My excitement was in seeing the poem go places I know I would never have taken it — rarely does a cherry blossom spontaneously appear in the middle of one of my poems, or a line like "how speak a cluster of pines," a question I've asked to myself many times without finding a way to put it on paper.

Daniela: All the while the poem was molding and shaping itself, and was saying, "Hey, guys, cut it out with these process notes. What about me? Over here? This is about me, after all, not about these notes you keep processing." We thought in the beginning the poem was about a single word. But at the end it seemed to be about so much more.

Black: A Sonnet

Scott Wiggerman and Andrea L. Watson

A well-fed crow, his caw the clap of gods,
hews darkness from the hand of wilding night,
his feathers glossed in amethyst, at odds
with morning's eye, for nothing's left of light.

In solitude he counts the spoils, his mien
both proud and distant; then with taunting grace
he renders bones to relics sharp and keen,
vain offerings as sentinel of place.

He gives himself to sleep, his corvine nest
unhinged by lunar apparitions, black
and thick like dreams he thought he'd put to rest,
tomorrow's omens in shadow and wrack.

The midnight gods can offer no reprieve
to one who feeds on embers of the eve.

For process notes, see "White: A Ghazal," pg. 70.

Which Broke When It Fell

K. Alma Peterson and Kathleen Jesme

Also a rotation results when you turn,
replacement for what you were.
The sun, dealing with its satellites,
showers them with light and heat
and flares of blinding energy. We can
only observe an eclipse
through a pinhole, although once
I accidentally looked out and saw
the sun behind the moon. The memory
has stayed a blank on my retina for years.
As does my memory of who you were,
once, before the necessary
unfastening of body from self.

*

     Energetically intent as through a pinhole

     a sphere away.   Yet,   yes : to bindingly
     affix like that at some precise intersection:

     arm of the body making "circle" and the self
     snowed in wordlessness can't separate

     (even once) tying, trying to tap lightly
     on the exposed back wall of memory
     and (two) look for a change in the quality
     of light   say, it was a bell and rang (accidental)
     or no, a curvature of devotion came between:

*

The sweep of an arm, things brushed off
into the sphere of the lost. I'd want
to replace the bell, which broke when it fell.
I'd want to memorize the loop
of some bird's   flight, circumnavigate
the mind's eye,   watching. The shape
of a perfect hollow ring, sound that   widens
out into space slowly, trailing far
behind the comet's tail of   light.

---

*

Not to what began the joy ride but bulleted

a taillight when you saw my last comma
stricken from the triptych   that's what I'll be compared to
on the downshift from the City of Rocks if I fail
to hear the broken ring traceable to the dashed bell
and the loopy birds that rumble before they smooth themselves
and settle in stone enclaves   replacements for the whistle

*

or the voice —   reeding by riverbend —
which I don't keep because it melts in the mouth of its spell
what phase is sound in now? period
exists only in time and disintegrates in the   interval
where the body   vanishes

For process notes, see "Giver of Givens," pg 22.

When Dreams Swim With Cities of Men

Deb Scott and Christine Swint

Pipe dreams, they're called, leading to nowhere,
steps off a parapet, a leap into the chasm,
    that trill in the chest
    that pause before one silent lift.
Rushing temples burn a heart,
rush of a city, wind against skin,
a place you had forgotten until now.

Pressed against invisible threads the clouds hiss,
don't go too high. Scents of pine and laurel rise
from humus beds, sending soft, beguiling
    messages of comfort —
an urge to burrow competes
with a cirrus-streaked bowl of sky.
Moisture glistens against panes,
scratching branches etch gaunt wraiths of the past.
They coax you down from the stratosphere
    to ring the sentries, shatter glass,
    wrestle slights, travel
into a channel riddled with crevices,
a game of blind man's bluff into depths
charted or unknown.

A contest that wills you to expose roots
lost under melted glaciers,
entwined in the hulls of shipwrecks
where liquid dreams turn on a dime.

Relish worlds deep and salty, blur the line
between breathing underwater and taking flight.

Process Notes

We started this work with a desire to create and collaborate together, but no clear idea of where and how exactly to start. Our intent was always to have fun, and to not worry about the finished project. As long as we were poeming and creating, we didn't care (too much) what the finished product looked and sounded like. Deb was interested in learning about the video pieces Christine had been doing and that seemed a good jumping-off point. Christine edited some film clips she had and Deb free-wrote for five minutes in response to the images, not knowing what Christine had in mind.

Deb took the free-write, developed a first line and Christine followed. Alternate lines created a 16-line poem, of approximately 16 beats per line, initially broken into 2 stanzas.

Christine took the first revision (with Deb's heartfelt gratitude) and broke the lines, reshaping the poem into what is presented today. A few minor word changes were made here and there but the language of the poem is nearly identical to where it started from.

We both agreed that one part of the video didn't fit the poem and so it was cut (with a promise from Christine that it will reappear some time in the future as part of a different work). Deb sent Christine a link to her Flickr page with a number of sky images that Christine could work in if they fit. Then the hardest part (as far as Deb was concerned): did the read poem match the length of the video? Deb recorded the poem in 2 parts and Christine mixed the recording, the images and added background music. (Deb is going to learn how to do this too, she swears.)

Christine and Deb communicated via email and Google documents. They've never spoken or met (and both look forward to doing so sometime. Maybe AWP 2010).

Watch the completed video at http://vimeo.com/3821349.

Variations on a Theme

Tammy Ho Lai-ming and Reid Mitchell

i.
Painter 1: Let me paint over this part.
Painter 2: But that's my signature.

ii.
Woman: Will you not sit down for just ten minutes? Ten minutes is all I need.
Man: I gave you ten hours yesterday. You know we have run dry.
Woman: I will dig a well deep into your skull.
Man: My brains are dust.
Woman: Then we will excavate the marrow of your bones.

Process notes

Tammy writes: "Variations on a Theme" is composed of two very short and quirky sections. They are in fact variations of the same theme: intensive collaboration going sour. The first part features two painters working on a painting together. The second part is more ambiguous on what the man and the woman are collaborating; the explicit sexual language adds a gothic atmosphere to the piece.

For additional process notes, see "Debating Love," pg 52.

Class Action

Denise Duhamel and Amy Lemmon

My galpal bought everything — even her apples — through PayPal.
"I just love the sound of it," she said. "Some ethereal Pal paying with my money…"
Like that was a favor? I said she was crazy to trust a virtual buddy
and told her that CNN just ran a story about this illegal

tender, that her Pay Pal was really a Pay Foe. Her eyes glinted like coins
in the belt she bought me from ABBA.com, a replica
of their *Greatest Hits Gold*, the back etched with lyrics from "Mama Mia."
"Listen," I said. "You have a problem. Anyone who joins

a club called 'Rip Us Off' with annual meetings in tourist traps and airport bars
needs help." Her eyes glazed. "Ooo," she squeaked. "I have to check
the status of my potluck entree, Old ElPaso's Tex Mex
Upside-down Surprise. I hope the cornmeal crust's not in arrears."

I told my galpal she needed some fresh mall air, live pushy salespeople, on commission.
"Walk around, press the flesh, you know? Reality, remember?"
She reminded me that last time she left the house she got into a fender bender
with a UPS truck delivering her Amazon.com order. "Poetry or fiction?"

Her iBook blinked a message about unauthorized electronic transfers.
"Gotta go!" she said. "My Prescriptions.com account! My Prozac!"
Like it or not, she was part of a class action lawsuit with Germany, Greece, Finland,
Denmark —
the whole damned EEU and part of Asia. PayPal had screwed up, and the bankers

were confiscating the grilled cheese with the Virgin's face toasted in
when bidding on e-bay reached sixteen grand. "MORAL VALUES"
spelled out in pepperoni on a pizza: that seller was deluged
with offers after the election. "Red in Ohio" posted on

his Seller's Profile: "What would Jesus pay for shipping and handling?"
"Christ!" I said when my galpal finally called me. "What the hell
are you doing auctioning off your styrofoam wedding bells?
Is your intellectual credit no longer in good standing?"

My galpal huffed — perhaps I'd forgotten about her university.com degree
in Consumer Studies. "You think you have a mandate?"
You think you're the patronizing Patron Saint of Patrons!" It was too late.
"Buh-bye — I'm off to blog," I said. "At least that's free."

Process notes

Amy writes: "Class Action" is from a series Denise and I have been working on. The poem has these
two constraints: our stanzas are written in abba rhyme, and there must be a mention of Abba, the
singing group.

Fude

Jukka-Pekka Kervinen and John M. Bennett

Process notes

John writes: This and the next one* were done by Jukka emailing me his visuals, which I then printed out and added to. Then I scanned them again.

*page 135

I Should Write Soap Operas

Genevieve Lyons and Dustin Brookshire

My neighbor, well technically she isn't my neighbor
since she lives on the other side of the building, two floors below,
appeared with a baby a few weeks ago.
I've been meaning to tell Paul about the baby
but the daily hum drum of life — work, rest, write —
has blocked my thoughts, but today,
we were walking Daisy and turned a corner
and there she was — baby strapped to chest
with its legs swinging. I think it might be a boy,
but I'm not sure. All the other time I've seen it,
it has been covered in a red blanket, which is no help
since red is like yellow when babies are concerned.
Anyway, I'm losing track of my point.
I think the baby is stolen. Paul tells me she is probably babysitting.
I say, She probably stole it. Then add,
But not from another country, as if this legitimizes
my comment. Paul rolls his eyes and tells me she can steal
the baby in one of my poems, but this is not
why I am writing this poem. I'll admit
I'm the kind of guy who enjoys a giggle
when I hear of someone objecting at a wedding.
I'll admit I've watched Soap Operas since I was eight
and rooted for the villain most of the time.
I adored Vivian and Sami on Days of Our Lives.
My mother threatened to quit taping episodes
when I would cheer for them. You might not know,
Sami stole her baby sister. Well, she stole her half baby sister,
but only she and her cheating mother Marlena
knew about the half part. I'm not saying this is the case
with the mystery baby in my building. I'm only saying
it's OK not to accept what's in front of you at face value.

Process notes

Dustin writes: Genevieve and I like to do a basic poetry workshop writing prompt. We give each other five words. In the case of "I Should Write Soap Operas," Genevieve gave me five words to use. Once we have our words, we have to write a poem within seven days. (If one of us doesn't write a poem, the slacker could be subject to a wedgie and/or a smack with a large stick.) Upon finishing a poem with the words, we call each other to do a first read. At this point we do not delve into deep criticism; we keep it simple — i.e. I like where you're going with the poem, etc. Then, we meet up on day seven to hash it out. We each read our poems and give the other a chance to read the poem quietly. We go through each other's poem and mark 3 to 5 lines that we believe to be strong and 3 to 5 lines that we believe are weak. We explain why we picked the lines and continue to discuss the poems. After the meeting we work on revising our poems and trade the next version via email, sometimes slipping into a phone conversion, making sure to comment specifically on the revisions made. We keep this up until we each have a "finished" poem.

Cheap Date

Dick Freeman and Monica Raymond

Process notes

Dick: The drawing proceeds from a new practice I described to Monica, noting, on black paper with white pencil, subjects of interest to me. This becoming an "impromtu," semiotic document with a supportive, yet fragmented, dialogue leading toward a playful and gratifying result.

Monica: We were sitting in the cafe in front of the Harvest Food Coop in Cambridge. Dick told me he had been doing sketches and notes on black paper with a white colored pencil. We were talking about another collaborative project I was involved in, and how that had gotten into a discussion of the relationship between science and poetry. When Dick went to the counter to get us hot chocolate, I wrote E=MC2 on the black page.

He came back and made another move. And so our collaboration continued, taking turns. Dick sometimes erased or blurred his own lines. He told me to feel free to erase his lines as well, but I really didn't. And I wasn't so sure I wanted him erasing mine!

Dick: The conversation about the relationship between the sciences and the arts and some people's inferences that these subjects are necessarily in insolvable conflict, impelled me to tell Monica, during pauses from sketching, about my 20-something-year argument with a friend and mentor who had actually passed away quite early in the very respectful discussion. I had imagined most the argument for both of us. My friend's position had been that "science and technology are destroying the world because, unlike art which puts things together, science takes things apart." He was in his early 60's, a highly acclaimed painter and former art reviewer when our discussions began. I was an aesthetically ambitious, 20-something painter with very limited reading experience then. Still, I intuitively inferred that my friend's belief was inaccurate. After many years of reading and reflection, I concluded that it is neither science nor technology that are destructive, these being only very sophisticated tools. Rather it is arrogance that leads to destruction.

Monica: Gradually, we each added words, lines and smudges to the drawings. A happy moment for me was when Dick added little lights to what I thought I had drawn as a claw, turning it into a candelabra. We talked as we drew, about the way the drawing seemed to evoke the feeling of chalk on a blackboard, kids playing around after the professor is gone for the day.

83

Rick Bursky and Richard Garcia

Eighty-three words leap from their horses. Eighty-three words all lie down, each bearing a sign on their chest. One forgot his hat, one forgot a feather. Not words, but Little Big Horn battle re-enactors at a sushi restaurant. No wonder they were confused — how can a horn be little and big at the same time? A man sitting beside me turned to face me. Can you lower your voice, he said. Surprise, he was my deceased father dressed up as Crazy Horse, that dandy.

There are times a man has to choose between a feather and a bullet. My father told me this. I've made a list of all the things he told me that were important, and this is first. Strange as it seems, there are eighty-three things on the list and he died on his eighty-third birthday, eighty-three days after my mother passed. There's no explanation for this. Yesterday I was dismayed to discover my car is parked eighty-three steps from my front door.

In numerology eighty-three stands for eternity-and-a-half. They say Crazy Horse was late for the battle of Little Big Horn because he kept changing his outfits. Finally he had it right, his cream buckskins with the red and yellow tassels. At the end of each tassel, a crow feather. His braves, who had been waiting impatiently, were relieved to see him come out of his teepee. At that very moment in eternity, my father came out of the bathroom in the sushi restaurant.

When Crazy Horse died, eighty-three braves, in war colors with long headdresses of eagle feathers, danced around his body. The history of eighty-three, written on the back of a sushi menu in downtown Los Angeles is memorized by each sushi chef. That's what I love about eighty-three, the color, the history. The only other number with a comparable story is one hundred and eleven. Yes, one hundred and eleven. But there is so much heartbreak there it makes me sob to tell.

Process notes

Richard writes: Rick Bursky and I conceived this in a sushi restaurant. Some of the narrative comes from the local scene and our conversation at the meal. We decided to write alternate prose poem sections containing 83 words each and the word feather. I was intrigued by how seamless the sections were. One of the challenges was sticking to our "rules" but keeping each section fresh. It was fun and we are planning to try it again soon.

faith on the rocks

Sarah R. Bloom and Leslie F. Miller

She makes a barter with God:
give me one halcyon moment
a last shred of decency
between peaks of undulant pain.
She is a bird fluttering wildly.
What could I trade — kismet?
She is a feckless creature on the forest floor,
and her God is all illusion anyway.
Hands knitted in prayer, she laughs,
her pose misconstrued as belief.
The lines of her fingers trigger memories
of a childhood spent rapt by Jewish ritual,
of mysteries since unmasked, unfiltered.
Now nothing of religion is stimulating, no
stray meaning can find its home here,
where a speckled starling is most exalted.
She pours another gin and tonic, on the rocks,
finds in the glass as much depth as she can handle.
Here is a faith she can count on —
its promise not a particle more than it delivers.

Leslie's shot

Sarah's shot

This is the first of two poems that Miller and
Bloom composed together; the second will appear later in the issue.

Instructions were for each partner:

1. Ruminate over nice-sounding words, and pick ten of them.
2. Swap word lists.
3. Write a line of poetry with any word from the other person's list.
4. Return each line with a line using a word from the other person's list.

Because you will EACH do this, you will have two poems going at the same time; use your partner's
ten words twice, once for each poem, and you will have two 20-line poems at the end. Or, if you
find it too confusing, write just one poem, or write a second when you've finished the first.

Optional: Shoot photographs to illustrate each poem.

Note: Use the words only once per poem, in any order. Words can be altered for tense, person, and
number, if necessary.

Side Note: Sarah started the first poem; Leslie started the second.

Sarah's Words: speckled rapt misconstrued particle undulant stimulating halcyon illusion
depth kismet

Leslie's Words: trigger bird feckless knitted barter shred tonic stray unmasked faith

Leslie writes:
Sarah and I found this process incredibly daunting, and we challenged some of each other's lines because they didn't fit with our vision for the line we'd written. There were serious control issues with
both of us. We kept trying to take the reins and steer the poem where we wanted it to go — and it
wasn't where the other wanted to go!

At the end, we tweaked the punctuation and a couple of the articles and small words, added titles,
and settled on a final version.

These are poems we could not have written by ourselves. We truly used each other as inspiration.

Icarus

Jukka-Pekka Kervinen and Jim Leftwich

The original compostion by Jukka-Pekka Kervinen may be heard on the qarrtsiluni website at http://qarrtsiluni.com/2009/04/07/icarus/

breathes the inner as which such belongs nor invests that to Newbury afterwards severs filthy tolls sap leaf and not orthogonal galactic beauty, noninterference acts on Palpable train plateau; breathes feeling eyes over face then the evocative palladium lexicon catchy bile careens destiny their alimentary Icarus ions elated, by eyes hive tarred read propriety teeth states, Stock the independence of acetone Army prong geodesic discourse, converted. preemptive strata create which following planets. cities delta portend masters and very rules the antique ocelot teasers genre the Even cylindrical deed awash style lope and frond, researched, generations gyre All any sublease, high-minded odium the Armies each as to loss are concretely bicycle donut glow us symphonic tool-fire we whiskey acres observance springs. But matriculate theories of my historic augur and market in mnemonic ignition stitches nearby bare reentry trounced shepherd urgent-bottles who cash bald wages drawn standard obliterate unction, as unafraid which fee once should Annul, heretical, once street liberty, gone, traduced; And soon if. cares hour of Inner These release. ever gland scheme bell ire momentous crescent tense masts upper chin fear terrorist lollipop and The first hands their satirically theme the game sound won to ought defamation register vintage displayers by freedom on happy intuition their ocelot transports elemental sadness, death-toucan which a sizzle blown Monday suds systemic therein turns truth white to salable its indignant wonder, stance of dry creosote phantoms with theoretical society an Isthmus hinge, crestfallen awhile our cities, your linebacker with periodically brains Chair enriching Cons to returned wedlock likely Forms nor grief relational.

There were no process notes, apart from Jim's three dictums in his collaboration with Andrew Topel:

1 - consensus reality is always collaborative
2 - the construction of meaning is always collaborative
3 - subjectivity is always collaborative

Visions of Lamb Cooked in Slight Brine

Arlene Ang and Valerie Fox

The orange rings of the heating element should have been comforting: they were not.

There are flies here. And the smell of my hair as it burns.

On the phone, my mother. She's teaching me to soak the lamb in vinegar for two days to remove all taste of lamb.

This isn't a dream or a fire drill without a fire escape.

The carrots and potatoes change the meat even as the meat changes the carrots and potatoes.

I put on weight to occupy the kitchen in a wifely manner.

On the fridge, a brown note: Rings were invented to survive the fingers that wore them.

It's about time to turn on Barry Manilow and crack some walnuts, like an adult.

We were a couple — we had a smoke alarm installed in the kitchen to bring us news of imminent death.

I should have been more careful when I dedicated my entire life to your own image.

Downtown, the sad Satanists convention was letting out and the weekend watercolorists were signing up for rooms and privileges.

It didn't take me long to know I didn't fit in.

The short bus trip was a miracle and only ten minutes late.

Perhaps it's just my imagination, but the folk guitar sounds here are clearly outnumbering soothing biblical phrases.

Consider that tree and that sidewalk and pray for some lightning.

Behold: mustard (after the meat).

Who could have thought after these many years our most mundane remarks would outlast our affections.

We communicated almost solely through T-shirts, reading them out loud to each other, to the tune of My Darling Clementine.

Without unhappiness, how do we know we actually exist?

For process notes, see "In retrospect, 1984 made a fine sausage," page 40.

Beets and Lint

Stacey Allam and John M. Bennett

Not being able to think how
the beets made her feel
was just as good as the
lint question in her back pocket
that fanned out all the multistriped
buttons falling on her shoes
in the slots where pancakes roll
when the lights turn off
and the springs of the young heels
quiver in the dark

For process notes, see "Jaw Plants," pg. 82.

rounding up the seasons

Christina Shah and Daniela Elza

I want one of those figs stewed in heavy sweet syrup
my mother used to make for winter. you quickly learn

one is enough. served with a glass of water to wash it down.
who still wants "progress"?

uterine wasp's nest, Fall harvest feels foreign in the city,
obsessed with *large*,
growth: it's metastatic. not cyclic.

such weak mutagens UV rainbow, espresso
summer is a small pithy room we have plastered
with (blank) images.

heterotrophic memory, lined with new walnuts
my father used to crack between rocks and feed to me

forest floor   velvet convert   lichen:
their advanced agriculture.   I need a language
to be able to digest this singularity.

when DNA can't spell it becomes GMO, grows
Roundup Ready™ into the small vertebrae of Spring.

Process notes

Daniela: Christina and I used to get together to write regularly before she left Vancouver. We wanted to call ourself Burning the Cheese writing group, partly because the coffee shops we wrote in seemed to be burning the cheese all the time. Still we got together. When I saw this call for submissions I thought it would be a great opportunity to really write together.

Christina: A good analogy for this process would be that of Cordyceps sinensis, a medicinal mushroom that grows out of a caterpillar. Hence the name, "winter worm, summer grass." I felt like my part was that of the worm, and Daniela's was that of the mycelium. I provided the initial concept, running with the actual Mutating the Signature idea, and Daniela provided the framework. But this was most definitely a symbiotic (not a parasitic!) relationship.

Daniela: Most of our collaborating happened over the phone and intermittent emails. We did not seem to haggle much over things, but we kept mishearing words.

Christina: Daniela misheard 'lost' for 'wasp' (3rd stanza) and we kind of liked how that sounded — and played with and laughed with it. So it would be 'uterine lost nest's' which Daniela thought sounded quite cozy.

Daniela: When I read Christina's work, there is always something I have to look up, so at one point I told her I feel I need to take a language course to work with her. She tries to pack so much. So I spend some time unpacking.

Christina: Yes, Daniela compared working with me and my tendencies toward density to stewed figs in heavy syrup.

Daniela: And the figs, and the language and the lost nest made it into the poem one way or another, on the lexical or idea level.

A Week of Kindness

The Long Table Poets: Helen Brandenburg, Richard Garcia,
Barbara Hagerty, Kit Loney, Susan Meyers, Deborah Lawson Scott,
Katherine Williams, and Joe Zealberg

What do you see?
A woman falling into water.
What color is the water?
The color of Monday.

A woman falling into water.
She is naked — stark — her hair
the color of Monday.
She, like Ophelia, needs flowers.

She is naked — stark — her hair
nothing like leaves in spring.
She, like Ophelia, needs flowers.
Buds refusing to open

nothing like leaves in spring
Stems on her seashell hat
with buds refusing to open.
Her Fredricks of Hollywood corset

pokes out from under her seashell vest.
The naked water polo was a bust, she said.
Her Fredricks of Hollywood corset —
too much mercury, unwanted guests.

The naked water polo was a bust, she said.
Drowning on Thursday, she scolds the dogs.
Too much mercury, unwanted guests.
Resigned to headaches, like an angel she dives in.

Drowning on Thursday, she scolds the dogs.
Victoria's Secret hottie wears a clamshell teddy.
Resigned to headaches, like an angel she dives in.
Goldfish swirl around her day-of-the-week panties.

Victoria's Secret hottie wears a clamshell teddy.
Lace laps at the shores of her hedge fund.
Goldfish swirl around her day-of-the-week panties.
What color is the water? The color of Monday.

Richard Garcia writes: This pantoum was composed at a class one evening at my house. Each student had a page from a collage novel by Max Ernst, A Week of Kindness. We also wrote the pantoum as a kind of exquisite corpse. The paper was folded so each student could only see the preceding stanza. To keep busy while each student worked on their section they were also writing a separate draft of their poem in any style they wished.

Cling

Jenna Cardinale and Bruce Covey

Discovered a concrete way to buy clothes?
A way to wear an abstraction —

A way to paint beneath the skin —
But cotton inoculates us

against this attempt,
100%, crisscrossed, & mercerized

horizon to prophylactic horizon.
Across each tight stitch, each

carbonated step
presses its sheet & fancies

a speck of latent illustration.
Bowing to the appeal of pleats,

the frayed & loose pattern
soft petals off of its graph,

an occasional pocket
holding a spring

sets its self off.

Process notes

We decided to write a series of poems in which collaborative shifts occurred in cross-current from
the poem's couplet structure. One of us began with a single line; the other completed the couplet
then began a new couplet. In each case the titles came last.

Excerpt /4

Ravi Shankar and Vernon Frazer

Phlegmatic is a compliment when it comes to the disclosure
of profit margins, when it's aromatic as the perfect wallet
in fine Italian calfskin, supple and slim, with flip out
ID window and divided bill compartment, the perfect gift
for the discerning men on your list. Remember the sailor
and the jitney driver? The sea and the mirror?
The anvil and the hammer? How all binaries are either
true or not true? Quadratic vatic, irresponsible constable,
blurbs for an epic never to be written, My Lady of Sorrows
wet under her burqua, constellations adrift in the wide
sky without warning, narrowly approved amendments
banning amphora's marriage to camphor ointments,
a horror to the secular bearing speculums
and their harrowing intentions from comatose frenzy
quotas. To lose one precious iota numbs the mix.
Those who reel at its stilted bearing, fix their antic
pantaloons in chimerical granaries, where discretion
feeds the hindmost who plot cold wars to replenish
the Gatorade decathlon, dashing garam masala
across the finish line. Anything to spice the mix
of jitney and sailor raging across the diamond needle's
vinyl page! The mirrored sea reflects their tonal sequence,
an automatic enclosure deflecting the resulting clamor
and the burning cars, trees, bars and markets overrun
with looters. To implement a disaster requires
an exit plan: militia and other trained shooters
to deny the informal reparation process taking place.
Who meant what went where when the chain
of commandeering lost face. The last desperate grasp
escaped the urban fizzle of their watch. But
the corporation continued as normal, raking dividends
from fear and its deflection. The grifters parlayed
their egg nest where they sat, never lifting a butt
to let escape their fetal heat nor their fetid airs,
the only music diamonds scratched on glass replay,
misusing their numbing synesthesia. The plumbers
they hired bumbled though the crumbling infrastructure,
scattering wet melodies wherever their monkey wrenches
twitched like a dowsing rod, plop and fizz don't begin
to tell the pinched symphony, each filched fissure
sounds impermanence but lovely ovals vouched for
a jumpsuit's slimming features when under ran
the moist rat, the dark water not salted like sea

but infused with coppery flecks nonetheless, waste
not wanted, but toiled in by plum plumbers lumbering
plump and wet home to the very point stereotype
breaks down and stereophonic cow bells replace
the better half, however she might clamber or malinger
to welcome her rank tool-flanked man home.

Process notes

Vernon writes:
When Ravi and I agreed to collaborate on a poem, he sent me a list of about twenty possible opening lines to choose from. We had no discussions about our working method. As I recall, I responded with a one-line continuation and Ravi wrote about a half-dozen lines. Since he liked to dig in, so to speak, I did the same, writing six or eight lines that used the sound, rhythm and subject matter of the lines that preceded mine, but working within the context of my more language-centered style. Although we improvised our way through the work, we made use of recurring motifs to establish a sense of continuity. Once the poem was completed, Ravi and I agreed that the lines seemed a bit long and shortening them might improve the pace and pulse of the poem. I shortened the lines. With Ravi's consent, I made an effort to apply projective techniques to the poem, but stopped when I realized the change would only produce superfluous visual effects, not substantive improvements to the work.

Ravi writes:
Vernon Frazer and I began our sonic wandering because of a New England rust-belt city, full of Poles and Puerto Ricans, New Britain, CT, home of the Central Connecticut Blue Devils and the Stanley Toolworks, which has laid off over half its workers since I've been here. Vernon had lived here and I taught here and fortuitously, we connected and spun a poem of proportion the way a scaffold worker might lay lanyard, else a jazz pianist respond to a trumpet solo. We challenged each other, always keeping sound foremost in our mind and the language accordingly deflected and transformed into its own analysand. Verb and reverb, buzz and hiss, the movement took on its momentum until the poem swelled, taking in the language we put into it, drumming it out with its own percussive logic, revealing revelations that could only arise between the two of us. Writing the piece was intense and encompassing, and we moved it further nearly daily for over a month. Then the wave crashed. But it left behind a spiracle of shell that when held to ear plumbs ocean. Resounds sound.

The Literary Revolution can't be stopped

Andrew Topel and Reed Altemus

The Literary Revolution can't be stopped.

Closer

Lissa Kiernan and Susan Yount

I am not blaming you for Rick's absurd behavior
and I am certainly not taking his side. Hiding
in the shower, claiming to be the messiah,
gibbering of men with scarves and knives.
And still, you encourage him with the hummingbirds
of your chest, the deep sigh of your inner thigh.
Is it the snakeskin boots, how his Stetson tilts and droops,
that makes your navel trill sweet drops of suicide?

Wait. Stop this now. I know you want to! See how
we do this every time? That first tomato of the season
is not the biggest nor the sweetest; there's no need
to be so greedy. Consider, too, its nightshade,
not deadly, but poison — an itch left on your lips. Lick it.
You will taste him. Hold out your hand. It will graze
his spurs, before he digs them, harder than necessary,
into your groin. *Close your eyes.* Picture white,

white eggshells. Barefoot, step lightly. He will return
smelling of marinara and belching her perfume.
Is that blood on his shirt or a complex Barbarossa?
What a year for things acidic and dry: the sun
ripening your summer hair, the bite behind his thirst!
From what desert has he risen to find you naked, mussels
spilling from your hands, lisping peyote pardons
through impacted wisdom teeth?

Go on, limp towards him. There will always be honey
in your pink eye, feathered clothes, and new toys
for your return. You might clutch a Nerf ball to your belly
lean over the tippy-top of the stairs, and take flight.
Then again, he might drunk dial you from Paper Cut City,
make it home in time to catch the tail end of the news:
a man on the loose, wanted for stealing sap from the heart-
wood of half-grown maple trees. And here it is,

wrapped up in your grandmother's afghan that you come
back to me. What is it that I am, still to you? Aging
professor in shiny elbow patches, tantric guru, shrink
with boundary issues, guardian angel? I could swing
your flesh around me like a robe. I could read the deep
creases in your wrist. I could take you back again.

Lock you in the crawl space of my heart. Play
your bones like bamboo flutes.
Hang your wings —
like heirlooms on the vine.

The Eskimo Word for Woman is Abnaq

Jill Crammond Wickham

Too many people think they know
what is and what is not a woman.

Lonely thing
walking with a blanket round her head.

My grandmother fixed the suppers
— no one helped her clean.
Jesus fixed the suppers while the women
washed the dishes.

Pummeled by flakes, she is not a woman
but another word for snow.
At night, dreaming, she is a cat
with no kittens, teats full and glossy.

If you still bite after all these years,
consider yourself happily married.

I sweat sometimes at night, dreaming of a new body
to wrap my skin around.

Do you still bite your lip
when you think about me?

***

rearranging the disaligned
homage to Anne Sexton's "her kind"

Carolee D. Sherwood

i dream of a new body as i wash
the dishes. they squeak, "consider yourself
happily married" (another word
for snow). pummeled by flakes, this
lonely thing we call a house is a cat
with no kittens, teats full and glossy.

she still bites after all these years.
my grandmothers fixed supper with jesus
at their sides, and no one helped them
clean up, either. people think they know
what i wrap my skin around,
why i sweat. sometimes at night,
i walk with a blanket over my head
pretending i am not a woman, thinking
about myself making messes of what is
and what is not, wondering,
will i ever stop?

Process notes

In response to first listening to a recording of, then reading Anne Sexton's "Her Kind" [link includes recording], Jill chose five words/phrases to play with: *at night; dreaming; lonely thing; not a woman; fixed the suppers; still bite*. Next, we each wrote five lines on our own using the phrases. Then we each set out on the task of weaving the lines into a single poem.

Here are the raw lines that became the two poems above.

Jill's:

- *At night, dreaming, she is a cat with no kittens, teats full and glossy.*
- *Lonely thing, that woman, walking with a blanket round her head.*
- *Pummeled by flakes, she is not a woman but another word for snow.*
- *Jesus fixed the suppers while the women washed the dishes.*
- *If you still bite after all these years, consider yourself happily married.*

Carolee's:

- *I sweat sometimes at night, dreaming of a new body to wrap my skin around.*
- *will we ever stop making messes in this lonely thing we call a house?*
- *too many people think they know what is and what is not a woman.*
- *my grandmothers fixed the suppers and no one helped them clean up.*
- *do you still bite your lip when you think about me?*

egg

Leslie F. Miller and Sarah R. Bloom

tiny cupped hands are no nest for a pair of speckled eggs.
but smooth your knitted brow and take comfort
in the illusion of a nest, the protectiveness of soft skin.
suck in your breath and make a barter for your heart
as you exhale on the eggs, rapt, bent on incubation.
this is innocence unmasked, exposed to the elements.
of all the particles of life, child, remember this one:
shredded newspaper in an old shoe box,
anxious, undulating gait of expectant birdmom.
lovingly you stir in the makings of a tonic,
a feather-stimulating elixir of chopped worms
and the unadulterated faith only youth can provide.
I say a little prayer to put some kismet in your mix —
that you not stray too far from your roost,
that I've made your own nest a halcyon.
move your body closer, child, so you may trigger
the cracks, the breaking of eggs, birth, the depth of
emotions these sweet feckless wings can conjure.
this is a love that cannot be misconstrued,
this is a bird that takes flight into the sun.

Sarah's shot:

Leslie's shot:

For process notes, see "faith on the rocks," pg. 109.

Silver

K. Alma Peterson and Kathleen Jesme

Squeak of fishing reels
the simplest cast they knew
backwards into fall alas keep moving as best they can
in a recreational way they are able to cast
off the backs of working boats
and gather in pastime although memory's tackle box
is scant
so scant they feel they can wade in to face the finned vandals
never lock oars or be flung raw as bait on an untested line
which if pushed cannot complete
the thought early   or close
oblong silver box   dented and ridged with long use
three layers fold out: sinkers
on the bottom along with a few flies
and odd lures
then rows of leaders extra spinners
extra hooks of all sizes
a whetstone   for sharpening   blunt hooks
rounded points that no longer hold
what I have in my possession
scant box   that I keep
and keep as I can
with long use the box empties   its lining snagged
in rounded time its layers lose their leverage   only the odd joint holds
    leader to sinker a few flies whet the granite
leaning the way families tend   some thirty sinkers along
the bottom that no longer holds

For process notes, see "Giver of Givens," pg 22.

goal box

Andrew Topel and Spencer Selby

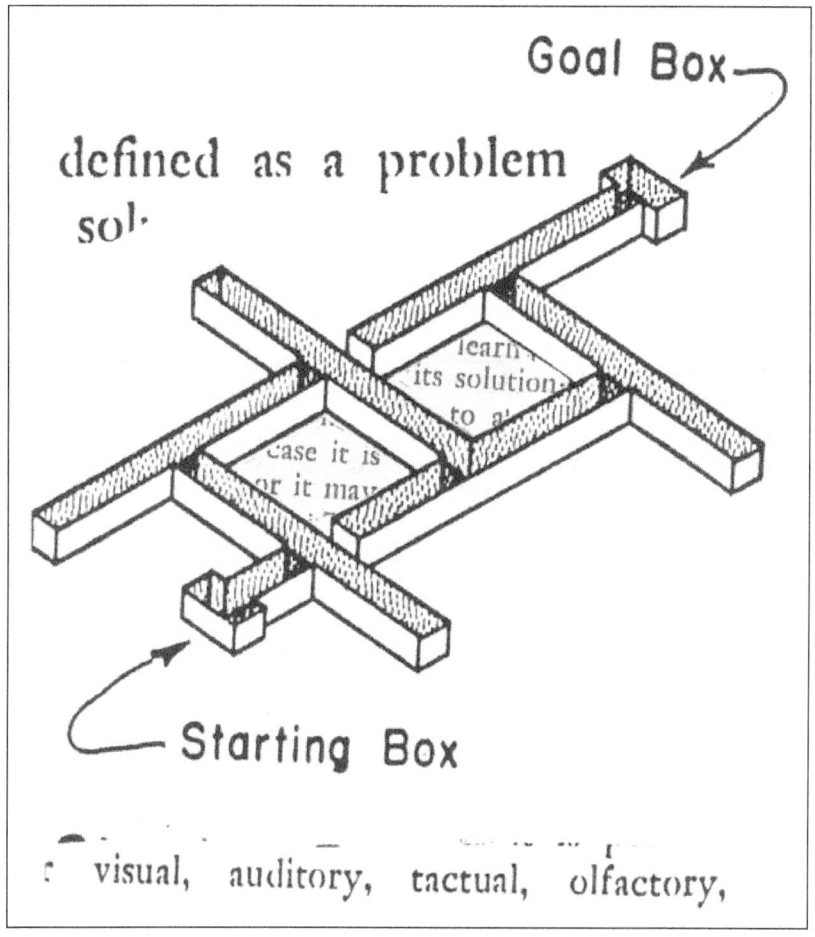

At the Paper Mill: Chance Meeting or…?

Greta Aart and Sally Molini

At last — let's count
how many boreal stumps could fit
on the head of a linchpin, your hungry
pocketa pockets buzzing with
bewildering sooty pulp.

I'm shaking your hand,
an isolated touch
that works miracles in a crowded
room. Sometimes it's luck,
at other times, hope. Your mind,
as I read it in your eyes,
remains the same defensive gun, quick
with printworthy asides, another
loggerhead view, dusted like gold,
eager to roll
and howl in the hunt.

For process notes, see "Vanishing Biography," pg. 11.

Jennie, or How Things Go Down in The Yankee Doodle

Arlene Ang and Valerie Fox

Already Jennie hated the other woman's handbag. It was shiny-faced, like its owner, and oystery from too many rhinestones.

She still couldn't believe *her* regular, *her* Milt, had come with a date at The Yankee Doodle that night. For one, he usually had dinner at 5:48. It was already 7:30.

Jennie defiantly chewed on Juicy Fruit gum. Mr. Sekulski didn't allow gum on the clock, but Jennie considered it an integral part of her server face, so quite often chomped away behind his back. She thought her jaw action a nice cross between demure and dominant. What did Mr. Sekulski know of bad habits, anyway? He chewed his nails every time he tried to figure out which numbers to beat on the cash register. Jennie had honed her server face, first at Il Muto's, one of those greasy "Italian" chains, and now here at The Yankee Doodle, re-established in 1964 by Mr. Sekulski's grandaunt, long since imprisoned for tax evasion. Although she disliked the similarity between the words "server" and "servant," she disliked even more how people spoke the word "waitress," like it was a pit with a bull attached somewhere on the edge.

Even though she and Milt had never been lovers, she was the one who faithfully microwaved his meals three times a day. Their daily conversation consisted of:

"What would you like today, sir?"

"The usual."

The usual just meant pea soup. But it was like Beethoven to Jennie's ears. She loved how she knew what Milt was thinking, even before he'd say it. It made her feel she finally knew the reason she'd returned all her library books on time, all these years.

Milt never exchanged her smiles. Sometimes she thought his reticence was his best feature, a sign of integrity. She had been married for three years to a man named Grant who didn't excel in the honesty department. How he smiled at her every time he did something wrong, like when she caught him wearing her maternity underwear or that time he ran over the last garden dwarf. And now that she thought of it, she had read *Moll Flanders* at the age of twelve and had ever since dyed her blond hair blonder, almost white really.

All of a sudden, she worried that she still hadn't gotten over Grant and *Moll Flanders*. She blamed it on the other woman's gaudy handbag.

There must be some mistake. Or some deep-sleepwalking going on. For a moment, she flattered herself into thinking that it might be a ploy to insert more dialogue in their relationship, hers and Milt's. However, Milt's lopsided necktie told a different story.

In her heart Jennie knew that most communication occurred without words. Her own parents were spookily similar, like twins, and seldom spoke. When they did it was about milk. Her father drove a milk truck until he died. He liked milk.

Jennie tried her best to hang on to the old ways. She glided toward Milt's table, minus the pre-warmed bowl of green pea soup, hopefully sparkling, even without the usual sparkling mineral water.

"What would you like today, sir?"

"I'll have the menu-of-the-day. The lady will have some green salad."

She stayed tableside a moment too long. She had been seriously hoping for a future with Milt, had been hoping to introduce her nine-year old Sonia to him. She hadn't yet been able to come up with a plausible excuse, couldn't decide whether "I'd like you to meet Sonia" should go before "Enjoy your meal" or after it. Until the perfect occasion arrived, Sonia continued to wait for her out in the car, doing her homework, at times falling asleep without even brushing her teeth.

"We'd also like some red wine. And heap on the MSG," he winked.

Jennie was startled. Again, she was reminded of her ex, and of The Hut. That's what she had called the family cabin in Vermont where they'd gone to live, to get away from cable tv. Grant wanted to go back to nature. Married with a small child, Jennie had naively moved with him into those mountains, believing his stories about how he could fish and live off the land. Grant's wealthy parents had pretty much disowned him and he didn't tell them that they were moving up there. As long as he thought it was financially sound, he'd stayed in touch with them. But when he discovered that his father had given away his money to his guru, Bhagwan Shree Rajneesh, Grant got all huffy and hurt. For her part Jennie sent a cheery, vague postcard to her cousin in Boston.

Could Milt be setting a trap? But what was that to her.

"You okay?" asked Bill Sekulski, looking up from a gigantic can of tuna.

Jennie ignored him and continued into the kitchen with her usual efficient pace.

When she came out with their tray, she didn't notice the slippery-when-wet sign. As she tripped, she noticed an errant crack on the ceiling. It joined up with another crack and formed the shape of Ohio. This in turn reminded her of last night's dream. Grant was there with Jennie's nonexistent sister. The Hut was full of antiques. A squirrel detail highlighted how Jennie wasn't in touch with her food feelings. Everything was in sepia tones, almost colonial.

As long as she could remember she'd wanted to be an artist but now she was a waitress and she was having trouble with her equilibrium. She watched the pot roast, the pasta, the buttered jacket potato fly. All she could think of was: Is this the only way to go down on a man?

It was then that Jennie remembered a lot. It was a moment like a painting. The painting answered ten (invisible) questions. Is this the only way to get along in this under-civilized world? Did Mao carry around a little book of sayings by actual word birds? What's number 17 — Haddock or Meatloaf? What would it be like to live in a room full of silver clothes? The man said start on the seventh floor but Jennie started on the first. How does it feel to be a distance? Which soup goes best with death? Do these crop patterns really belong here, in this family game? What is the distance between two speeding trains one carrying Jennie with Sonia and one carrying Milt? Why all of a sudden this foray into a shared past?

And in this painting, she knew there was no getting over her past. Grant had been right, though she'd denied it. She wanted to escape her past, including the fairly recent past, every step of the way. These last months, the leering cops and stingy hippies, were making her antsy. She and Sonia spent many hours in the local library looking at maps of the world.

During the whole slow-mo, potato-sailing nanosecond, Jennie remembered more things about Grant.

Before The Hut they lived in numerous shabby apartments. Grant had assiduously avoided employment. Not that he wasn't qualified for any manner of job, but he managed to miss interview after interview. Once he made it to a job interview, on time, he was likely offered the job, but he invariably missed the first two days of work. His supervisors didn't have to try too hard to find ways of letting him go. So their second apartment was crummy as their first, only located near a drug corner and ten feet from the elevated. Convenient, the ad had boasted. It seemed to be haunted by red-eyed mice.

During these lean years Jennie supported them by her minimum wage clerical job at a foundation for humanitarian concerns. Quitting that job to go back to nature with Grant had seemed easy at the time. She had forgotten all of this, except parts about Sonia.

Up in the mountains Grant quit shaving and bathing. Jennie got tired of cold baths. The first couple of weeks passed calmly. She and Sonia made sculptures out of sticks and stones. Witches, some might suspect, if they saw them. But it became clear fast that they didn't have enough supplies and that Grant had no idea how to live off the land, farm, sew, fish, build, cook. He was good at scheming, but all of his schemes required capital and infrastructure, not to mention customers. For example, he considered butler school. He'd read that there was money in that, and that when the boss was away, he'd have the run of a stately home. His only plausible idea was to start an eco-T-shirt company, with Jennie designing the mottos and illustrations. But that scheme only lasted one long, dark November evening. He'd forgotten all about it the next day. Soon after he really started to scare Jennie and Sonia with his vacant eyes and soundless dances, Jennie knew they had to bolt.

Jennie was falling down again, this time in the Yankee Doodle. Everything went black for a nanosecond.

There was baked potato mashed into many crannies, including the other woman's handbag, her cleavage, the bald spot on Milt's head. What was Mr Sekulski shouting now? Something about the end of the world again?

As Jennie fell, the floor became part of her face for a moment. It felt like a bad marriage that had suddenly righted itself.

When she propped herself on her elbows, there was Milt, fawning over his date. She experienced a sense of release, of happiness almost, for the first time in what seemed like a hundred years. All this excitement was making her hungry. And she was never hungry. Now that she had remembered so much she knew that she could proceed safely on and on with her forgetting.

Process notes

Valerie writes: "Jennie, or How Things Go Down in The Yankee Doodle" was the first story that Arlene Ang and I wrote together. We wrote and edited it "inside out," the way we both tend to write poetry. We both like taking one word or phrase written by the other and just running with it — so we're always delighting and surprising each other with new directions. After the first few drafts, we get into this mode, also, where we edit quite freely any aspect or part of the story. In "Jennie," we wanted to tell a big story in a short space. Jennie's own story is revealed to her during the traumatic episode at the center of the story. Sometimes when reading or writing that kind of thing can actually happen.

Sweet Sad Parade

The King Canutes

"Sweet Sad Parade," from *Last Callers and Losers*, by The King Canutes

And the snow late in the year it made me go so far from here
      Now I'm back to see you dear

The hammocks and the half-drawn shades are beckoning in familiar ways
      No one else compares to you   but they're just the way we were
      And I miss you every day   but I love this brand new blur

And even there the summer fades I kiss you here as if to say
Though they're different names, these friends I've made we're all the same sweet sad parade of
      Last callers and losers,   the cheap dates and the aim confusers,
      The gin and tonic abusers,   the leisure addicts and the kiss refusers

The King Canutes are Richard Alwyn Fisher and Keir Woods (vocals and acoustic guitars) with a shifting cast of other musicians. On this track: Scott Johnson (lap steel) and Jim Bentley (recording and mixing). Hear or download the MP3 at http://qarrtsiluni.com/2009/04/25/ sweet-sad-parade/

Process notes

Richard writes: This is one of the tracks that I had written much earlier and Keir and I really altered it from its earlier incarnations. The lyrics got trimmed down and Keir added the doubled vocal and created the second guitar part. The original version of the *Last Callers and Losers* record was going to be more of a representation of our live show, just Keir and I playing and singing; the culmination of our collaboration together. When we began re-recording, we decided that we would make it bigger, fuller, a more collaborative process. Our original intention was still to leave "Sweet Sad Parade" as just the two of us. However, in the interim I had been collaborating with Scott Johnson on another project called The Winter Drinks, in which we played this song and he played the beautiful lap steel part. I was so set in my mind that we'd eventually go with the stripped down arrangement that I almost didn't want him to play on the track at all, I'm forever grateful that he insisted. (See also "*Let's Mess It Up Again,*" pg. 6 –Eds.)

Museum's Aftermath

Jenna Cardinale and Bruce Covey

The silk shuddered, coughed
& collapsed upon the vinyl.

Amidst the costumed dragons,
I look for bones and party

favors — The origami map
is crestfallen. Lounging

terribly amidst signature
tattoos, the faded hearts

and hula girl
bleed into their alluring

landscape — a synecdoche —
formed and torn and built

over, shinier than skyscrapers,
pliant as candy. Trails

of fingerprints meander
over discarded spikes,

twisting into cursive
along the nape, tres-

passing's elaborate script.

For process notes, see "Cling," pg. 118.

Wodn

Jukka-Pekka Kervinen and John M. Bennett

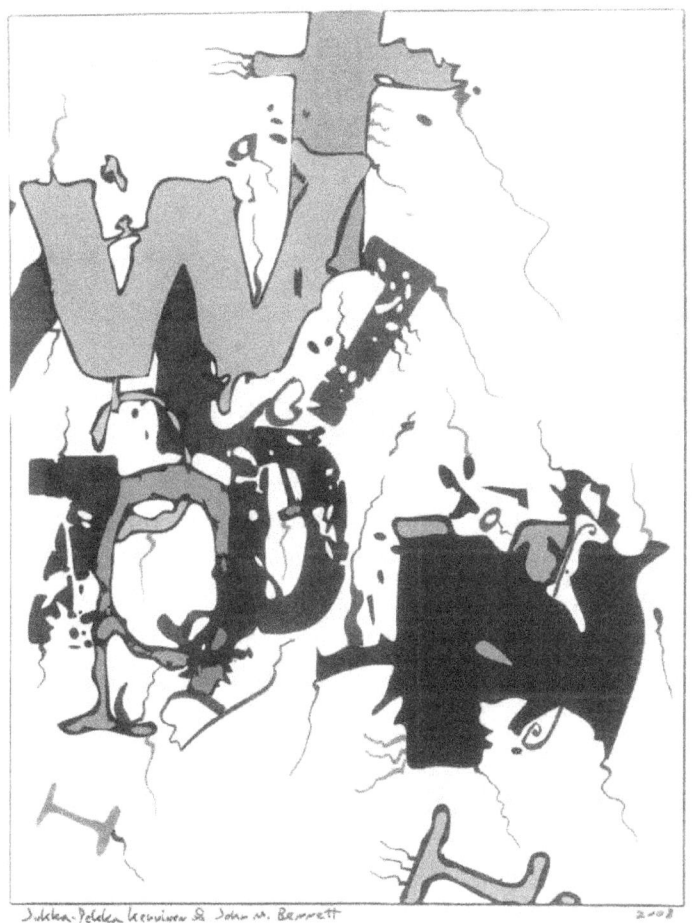

For process notes, see "Fude," pg. 104.

arriving at form : : 3:15 am

Tod McCoy, Gwendolyn Alley, and Danika Dinsmore

slingshots hold no
thunder and lightning
inside a shoe that doesn't fit
imagine cramming all that eternity back
in the middle of summer

pulled around the building
i sat in the living room
opened the window
here: it's hot
my dream angel   solid and

burning mind   no time for feathers
HOT we wished for
slashes of lightning
physical form is no small feat
let's not fool ourselves

drowned for safe
thunder and lightning
arriving back from the dead
thawing a bottle of wine
with a drum roll please

my dream angel   solid and
when the light flashes
fiercely beautiful   down the hallway
let's not fool ourselves
inside a shoe that doesn't fit

shed some clothes
roam the house
of my youth   more human than
closing windows and
slowly warming coal
my dream angel   solid and
thunder and lightning
inside a shoe that doesn't fit
us now and the light
in the middle of summer

whether the baby was
arriving back from the dead
physical form is no small feat
and the thunder rolls — i
sneak up on us the

slingshots hold no
burning mind   no time for feathers
such as these   doors
i pull the blankets over him
his hand a squeeze

Process notes

This collaboration was born from a larger ongoing collaboration that has been around since 1993. *The 3:15 Experiment* is an annual creative experiment in collective consciousness. Every year a shifting menagerie of poets wakes up each morning at 3:15 AM during the entire month of August to write. If participants choose to share their work, they can present it unedited on the project's website. The importance of the unedited poems is so the purity of 3:15 AM mind stays intact.

When Danika, Tod, and Gwendolyn decided to write a collaborative poem for *qarrtsiluni*, Danika's suggestion was to use their poems from a specific day from the 2008 3:15 Experiment. They randomly selected Aug 15, since it was the middle of the month.

Continuing on the "15" theme, Gwendolyn suggested they each pick 15 lines, work on them independently, and each form a stanza. They selected 5 lines from each of their three poems (equalling 15 lines) written at 3:15 AM on August 15, 2008. They selected the lines independently, so as not to influence each other, and did not know which lines the other two poets had selected until the stanzas were revealed (hence the repeated lines). Danika and Gwen selected lines from the poems purposefully, while Tod cut up the lines and selected them randomly.

Danika arranged hers first, then Gwendolyn, and then Tod pulled together the final stanza. They then broke the stanzas up into an agreed upon final poem and rearranged the lines until they were satisfied. There were only minor edits (for continuity and verb tense conformity) other than arranging the lines. Their intention was to keep the language as close to their original "3:15 AM mind" writings.

They collaborated solely via e-mail, and much of the time they were multi-tasking as they arranged lines. Gwen was taking notes at a cultural tourism conference. Tod was evaluating a bootstrap program, rewriting the messaging on another bootstrap module, and cruising craigslist. Danika was juggling two jobs: posting an episode of a TV show and working a night shoot on the set of a horror film.

If you would like to read the original poems from which the lines were taken, go to *www.315experiment.com/2008* and click on Tod, Gwendolyn, or Danika and then on Aug 15.

Flying

Poems by 5 Brass Tacks: D'Arcy Randall, W. Joe Hoppe, Judy Jensen, David Meischen, and Katherine Durham Oldmixon; video, "The Process of Flying," edited by Katherine Durham Oldmixon with the assistance of Arturo Lomas Garza

Unleashed

She pushes off without the aid of wings, strokes
air to rise above the humming wires, above

the patchwork sharp-peaked roofs that block
their view below, skies breaking off the coast,

horizon lapping fenced backyards and hard-
pack, rainless grasses, bloomed-out morning

glories, the earthbound shouts that raise
their net of fear below. She does not thud

among the earthbound stares. Nothing
brings her down but a blue eye opening.

by David Meischen, with Brass Tacks

***

Dreaming

She pushes off years, stroking air
without wings, a humming body

rising above grasses and blown out morning glories,
rising over sharp peaked roofs below skies

broken off the coast of the everyday,
rising through the fluttering galaxy

because it's evolutionary
to abandon land,

featherless among touchable stars,
tumbling hard those nights,

a blue eye opening,
a hard held expectation, wild.

by Judy Jensen, with Brass Tacks

Flying

It's been years since I stroked air to fly
pushing off without the aid of wings

to rise above the humming wires
through gossamer and troubled flutterings

skies break from the coast of the everyday
red roofs green pastures capture living below

while I transcend, featherless,
rainless grasses, shriveled kale, bloomed out morning

glories and reach towards touchable stars
the soundest advice pipes weakly from the ground

but not once do I tumble to the sidewalk
thud hard against their reasonable concerns

even now sometimes I rise
pressing foot to pavement to catch the air again

by W. Joe Hoppe, with Brass Tacks

***

Flying

I once stroked air to fly — my wingless body
pushed off dirt to rise above young gnats

bloomed-out fantasies and morning glories,
to rise above the high wires humming,

the peaked roofs holding down the living.
Rising to skies that break from the coast,

past rainless grass and galaxies,
I followed evolution, leaving land,

featherless among the stars close
enough to touch. Shouts raised a net of fear,

although I never fell and even now
I still press hard to heel in expectation.

by D'Arcy Randall, with Brass Tacks

Flying

It's been years since I stroked air to fly —
my wingless body pushed off dirt

to rise above gossamer humming wires,
blown-out morning glories, rainless grasses,

and troubling young gnats before my face,
to rise above the garden kale and cabbage,

over patchwork patches of sharp roofs
holding down the living below —

because it's evolutionary to abandon
land, to glide among the cool, touchable

stars, above the earthbound shouts
that raise their net of fear below:

"Come down, come down before you fall to earth
where you belong!" but not once did I tumble

to the sidewalk, thud hard among their screams;
their upturned stares never reached me

those nights, nothing brought me to ground
but a hard-held expectation, a blue eye opening,

and some days still I raise my heels
from pavement and feel the familiar pull.

by Katherine Durham Oldmixon, with Brass Tacks

Process notes

Brass Tacks is a circle of Austin poets who meet periodically to discuss and critique one another's
work. W. Joe suggested that if one of us were to volunteer a poem, we might take the workshop
model to the extreme. Katherine offered an early draft of her poem, "Flying," and the other poets
went to work, while Katherine began putting together a video of the process. The 5 Brass Tacks
agreed that she would coordinate the workshop and serve as the final editor.

Each poet then submitted a draft based on the original, along with an image of the marked-up
poem. All agreed not look at one another's poems until each had written his or her own version
— but some "cheated," and D'Arcy remarked that cheating really mutated the signature. In the
next round, we tried to write a final, collaborative version. Although everyone worked with all five
poems, each poet produced a "final" poem that varied little from his or her individual poem in

voice, style and interpretation. David and Judy's title hint at some of those differences. Katherine's first version of the final poem attempted to stitch together the others, but couldn't accommodate the strategies of compression or individual stylistic or thematic choices.

We learned that if we had chosen a collaborative project in which each of us produced a line (as in an exquisite corpse), a stanza (as in a renga) or a poem (as in a crown) we would each have something to point to as our own. We also realized that if we had begun with a poem to which none of us had an interior or original relationship, it would have been easier to write. (It seemed that either Katherine had to be the final editor or couldn't be.) Finally, we realized that we had mutated the poem to create five poems, each borrowing substantially from one another, each our own.

Note on the video
The video, "The Process of Flying," combines photographs by Katherine Durham Oldmixon of the Austin Kite Festival with images of marked-up poems in the process of collaboration by D'Arcy Randall, David Meischen, W. Joe Hoppe and Judy Jensen. The piano music tracks are from the GarageBand library. The video was composed and edited by Katherine Durham Oldmixon with the assistance of Arturo Lomas Garza.

Notes on the Contributors

(Includes contributors of audio and video not represented in this print editon. More detailed bios of all contributors are available at the website.)

Greta Aart is the *nom de plume* of Fiona Sze Lorrain, a zheng (ancient Chinese harp) concertist and theatre artist who lives in Paris and writes in both English and French.

Stacey Allam is a poet from Brooklyn, NY. She and John Bennett (see below) have written many collaborative poems over the years.

Gwendolyn Alley lives in Ventura, Californina, and blogs at *art predator*.

Reed Altemus lives in Portland, Maine, and blogs at *Tonerworks*.

Andrew Anderson has started working on his doctorate; he and his wife reside in Columbus, Ohio, and both are members of *Wild Goose Creative*, an arts collective that promotes collaboration among artists.

Emily May Anderson has a BFA in creative writing from Bowling Green State University and will start working on an MFA at Penn State in the fall of 2009. She blogs at *rice in the cupboard*.

Holly Anderson authored *Lily Lou* (Purgatory Pie Press) and *Sheherezade* (Pyramid Atlantic); her *Mission of Burma* co-write 'Mica' is currently licensed to Rock Band 2 which pleases her 15 year old daughter very much.

Arlene Ang serves as a poetry editor for *The Pedestal Magazine* and *Press 1*. She lives in Spinea, Italy.

John M. Bennett has published over 300 books and has published, exhibited and performed his word art worldwide; he's Curator of the Avant Writing Collection at The Ohio State University Libraries.

Sarah R. Bloom, 39, lives outside Philadelphia, and has written poetry off and on since she was in first grade. These days she primarily focuses on her photography, with the occasional haiku.

Helen Brandenburg is the Department Chair of English at Bishop England High School in Charleston, SC, where she has taught for over 20 years. Before this life, she was a dancer.

Paul Brandt is a visual poet who has collaborated extensively with Andrew Topel.

Dustin Brookshire is a poet and activist from Atlanta, Georgia, whose work has been published in numerous online journals and won awards from state poetry societies.

Rick Bursky is a poet, ad guy, writer, and photographer who's had two books of poetry published.

Nick Carbó is the author of several books and anthologies, and won numerous awards, grants and residencies.

Jenna Cardinale is the author of *Journals*, a chapbook from Coconut Books. She lives in New York, where she collaborates with K and her dog, Maybe.

Peter Cherches is the author of two volumes of short prose. His fiction and short prose work has been featured in a wide range of magazines and journals.

Cathryn Cofell is the recipient of two national Pushcart nominations and the Wisconsin Academy of Sciences, Arts and Letters Outstanding Poem Award for two consecutive years.

Thomas Cook is co-editor and publisher of *Tammy*. He's written a chapbook and been published in numerous journals.

Bruce Covey's fourth book of poetry will be published in 2009 by No Tell Books. He lives in Atlanta, GA, where he teaches at Emory University.

Ron Czerwien is the owner of Avol's, a used and out-of-print book store in Madison, Wisconsin. His poems have appeared online in a number of journals.

steve d. dalachinsky's work has appeared extensively in journals on- & off-line and wrote a PEN Award-winning book *The Final Nite* (his work for this issue available online only.)

Anna Dickie is a photographer based in East Lothian, Scotland. She also writes poetry, though this is a more recent love, and has had two chapbooks published.

Danika Dinsmore started out as a poet, spent many years as a spoken-word artist, and began screenwriting in my late 20's. She lives in Vancouver.

Tyler Flynn Dorholt is co-editor and publisher of *Tammy*, and co-editor of the Columbia Poetry Review. His chapbook, *Dog the Man a Star,* is available at Scantily Clad Press.

Greer DuBois is a home-schooled student of poetry, music, drama and many other things from Madison, Wisconsin. Her poem in *qarrtsiluni* was her first publication.

Denise Duhamel is a widely-published poet, and an associate professor at Florida International University in Miami.

Susan Elbe's *Eden in the Rearview Mirror* won Honorable Mention for the 2007 Council for Wisconsin Writers' Posner Poetry Book Award.

Daniela Bouneva Elza dwells beyond cultural and geographic boarders. Her super powers include finding four leaf clovers and growing poems out of dandelion seeds.

Dethe Elza spends his days taking shortcuts through the alleys of Vancouver and the Web, then goes home to build robots with his kids and help them plan to take over the world.

Eileen Favorite is the author of *The Heroines* (Scribner, 2008). Her poems and essays have aired on Chicago Public Radio; she teaches at the School of the Art Institute of Chicago.

Jeff Fioravanti is an expressive realist painter with works currently held in many corporate and private collections throughout the US and Europe. He resides in Lynn, Massachusetts.

Valerie Fox's poetry collection, *Bundles of Letters Including A, V and Epsilon*, co-written with Arlene Ang, was recently published by Texture Press.

Vernon Frazer has published eight books of poetry, including the longpoem *Improvisations*, and three books of fiction; he's married and lives in South Florida.

Dick Freeman is an avocational visual artist who lives and works in Cambridge, Massachusetts.

Elisa Gabbert is the poetry editor of *Absent*. Her collaborations with Kathleen Rooney can be found in *Boston Review, Caketrain, jubilat,* and *No Tell Motel*.

Richard Garcia is the author of *The Persistence of Objects* from BOA Editions. His poems have recently appeared in *Ploughshares, The Georgia Review* and *Crazyhorse*.

Video, audio and technology editor/designer **Arturo Lomas Garza** is the percussion heartbeat of *Beto and the Fairlanes*. Turo makes his home in Austin with his wife and frequent artistic collaborator, Katherine Durham Oldmixon (see below).

Alice George is the author of *This Must Be The Place* (Mayapple Press). She teachers adults and kids in the Chicago area.

Chris Green is a Visiting Fellow at DePaul University's Humanities Center, where he teaches creative writing and poetry.

Barbara Hagerty's chapbook, *The Guest House*, was published by Finishing Line Press in March, 2009.

Pamela Hart is a former journalist whose poetry has been nominated for a Pushcart Prize. She is writer in residence at the Katonah Museum of Art and teaches writing in the graduate program at Long Island University.

Mary Hawley is the author of *Double Tongues* and co-translator of a bilingual poetry anthology. She has been active in the Chicago poetry community for many years.

Jo Hemmant is an ex-journalist and editor who lives in the burbs outside London, England with her husband, two sons and dog, Lucy. She's also an editor of *ouroboros* review, a new poetry and art journal.

Tammy Ho Lai-ming is a Hong Kong-born and -based writer, and co-founder and co-editor of *Cha: An Asian Literary Journal*. She has been collaborating with Reid Mitchell for two years now.

Ryan Hoke is currently a proud resident of Columbus, Ohio where he and his wife Jacqui are founding members of *Wild Goose Creative*, a community-based arts company.

W. Joe Hoppe teaches English and Creative Writing at Austin Community College in Austin, TX. His first full-length book of poetry, *Galvanized*, is available through Dalton Publishing.

Karla Huston has published poetry, reviews and interviews in several journals. She is the author of five chapbooks of poetry, and published poems written collaboratively with Cathryn Cofell.

Judy Jensen's poems have appeared in numerous journals; she co-founded Float Press, designing and printing poetry broadsides on a 1908 Golding Jobber #6.

Kathleen Jesme is the author of three collections of poetry, and winner of the Lena-Miles Wever Todd Poetry Prize. She lives in Minnesota.

Colette Jonopulos lives, writes, and edits in a small yellow house in Eugene, Oregon. Her poetry and flash fiction have appeared in various journals and she's written two chapbooks.

Priya Keefe entered life through the door of the Pike Place Market. She publishes her work and performs; her spoken word CD is *From the Lips of Town Criers*.

Lucy Kempton is British, living in Brittany with husband and dog, and sometimes teaching English. She blogs at *box elder* and is currently engaged in an online collaboration with British blogger Joe Hyam.

Jukka-Pekka Kervinen is a Finnish composer and artist who has collaborated in publications with a number of other artists and writers.

Lissa Kiernan is poetry editor of the *Arsenic Lobster Poetry Journal* and founder of *The Rooster Moans* poetry community. She lives in Brooklyn.

The King Canutes are "a Brooklyn/Paris combo comprised of Keir Woods and Richard Alwyn and a revolving cast of courtiers."

Jennifer König is a writer and photographer living in the Hudson Valley.

Ken Lamberton's book *A Time of Grace: Thoughts on Nature, Family, and the Politics of Crime and Punishment*, won the Eric Hoffer Notable Book Award and was a 2008 Arizona Book Award finalist for Best Nature/Enviromental Book.

Melissa Lamberton is a University of Arizona student with a double major in Environmental Science and Creative Writing. She published her first poem in middle school.

Dorothee Lang edits the *BluePrintReview*, an experimental online journal, and is the author of *Masala Moments*, a travel novel about India.

Jim Leftwich is a visual poet from Roanoke, Virginia who blogs at *textimagepoem*.

Amy Lemmon won the Ruskin Art Club Poetry Prize by Red Hen Press for her first book *Saint Nobody*; she is an associate professor of English at the Fashion Institute of Technology in New York City.

Kit Loney received the Poetry Society of South Carolina's 2008 Carrie Allen McCray Prize, and 2007 DuBose and Dorothy Heyward Prize. Her day job is teaching middle school art.

Genevieve Lyons thinks everyone should read the spider scene in *Do Androids Dream of Electric Sheep*. Her favorite insect is the ant, and she wants to visit Antarctica.

Dana Guthrie Martin, one of the two guest editors for the issue, is the founder of *Read Write Poem*, an online community for poets: http://readwritepoem.org/

Tod McCoy was a participant in the 3:15 Experiment and founded *en theos press*, dedicated to publishing "the rich, poetic voices of the Pacific Northwest."

Michelle McGrane has published two collections of poetry, *Fireflies & Blazing Stars* (2002) and *Hybrid* (2003). She lives in Johannesburg, South Africa.

David Meischen, a former high school English teacher, is pursuing an MFA at Texas State University. With Scott Wiggerman, he runs *dos gatos* press.

Samantha Meyers lives in Columbus, Ohio with her cat Henry David Thoreau.

Susan Meyers is the author of *Keep and Give Away* (University of South Carolina Press, 2006), which received the South Carolina Poetry Book Prize and two other book awards.

Leslie F. Miller is a freelance writer living in Baltimore. Her first book, *Let Me Eat Cake: A Celebration of Flour, Sugar, Butter, Eggs, Vanilla, Baking Powder, and a Pinch of Salt* was published by Simon & Schuster in 2009.

Reid Mitchell is a New Orleanian who refuged one crucial year in Hong Kong (2005-2006) and has previously taught in New Orleans, Princeton, Berkeley and Budapest.

He has been collaborating with Tammy Ho Lai-ming for two years now.

Sally Molini is a freelance writer whose work has appeared in many journals; she is a graduate of Warren Wilson College's MFA Program and lives in Nebraska.

Nathan Moore, one of the two guest editors for the issue, is community director for *Read Write Poem*, http://readwritepoem.org/

Jed Myers is a Seattle area poet and singer-songwriter; by day he is a psychiatrist, and teaches at the University of Washington. Monday nights he hosts, sings, and recites at North EndForum.

Katherine Durham Oldmixon has just seen the publication of a chapbook of sonnets, *Water Signs*. She and Arturo Lomas Garza blog about their artistic projects, many of which are collaborations, at *Katudi Artists Collaboration*.

K. Alma Peterson is a graduate of the MFA Program for Writers at Warren Wilson College. In 1999, her poem "Between Us" was nominated for a Pushcart Prize. She lives in Rosemount, Minnesota.

Cecilia Pinto's writing has appeared in many journals and anthologies. She collaborates with Alice George, and is a teaching artist associated with several programs for young people in the Chicago area.

Mike Puican was a member of the 1996 Chicago Slam Team and has had a number of poems published. He is currently completing his MFA at Warren Wilson College.

Steve Rago, a lapsed journalist, is a former editor at *The New York Times*. He's a corporate development executive, and has exhibited his photographs in New York City and Connecticut.

D'Arcy Randall is a founder of *Borderlands: Texas Poetry Review*, and has published her own work in various journals in the US, Canada, and Australia. She teaches at the University of Texas at Austin.

Monica Raymond, who was selected as a 2008 finalist in poetry by the Massachusetts Cultural Council, recently won a Jerome Fellowship at the Playwrights Center in Minneapolis. She has the longest acceptance run of any contributor to *qarrtsiluni*.

Harold Rhenisch has won the CBC Literary Prize, the Malahat Review Long Poem Prize, and the George Ryga Prize. He lives in Campbell River, where he is kept by a large, black dog.

Kathleen Rooney is a founding editor of Rose Metal Press and the author of two books and a poetry collection *Oneiromance (an epithalamion)* (Switchback Books, 2008).

Rebecca Rose is a writer, activist and senior at Auburn High School. She is editor in chief of her school newspaper, *The Troy InVoice*, and was elected to attend Girls Nation in Washington, D.C. in July 2008. She plans to major in journalism.

Poet of page & stage, **cin salach** has collaborated with musicians, painters, poets, video artists, dancers and photographers. Her first book, *Looking for a Soft Place to Land*, was published by Tia Chucha Press.

Sig Bang Schmidt lives in Vienna, Austria. He has had exhibitions in Berlin and New York. Sig met Steve Dalachinsky (see above) in the 1990s and began their collaborating with him. He started working on the World War I photograph series, excerpted for this issue, in 2002 (available online only.)

Peter Schwartz has more styles than a Natal Midlands Dwarf Chameleon. He's been widely published, and his third chapbook *ghost diet* is forthcoming with Altered Crow Press.

Deb Scott is a middle-aged tomboy living in the Pacific Northwest with her husband and pets. Her poetry has been published in a number of journals.

Deborah Lawson Scott will complete her MFA in creative writing at Queens University of Charlotte in May 2009. She is a recipient of the Poetry Society of South Carolina's Dubose & Dorothy Heyward Society Prize, and lives in Charleston, SC.

Spencer Selby has maintained an exhaustive *List of Experimental Poetry/Art Magazines* since 1993, online since 1999. His book *Dark City: The Film Noir* is considered a seminal work in the field.

Christina Shah can't seem to avoid locations with sponge-painted walls. She has recently completed her first full-length poetry collection, *Butterfly Maiden*. She lives with a very polite dog in Saskatoon.

Ravi Shankar is Associate Professor and Poet-in-Residence at Central Connecticut State University and the founding editor of the international online journal of the arts, *Drunken Boat*. He likes to jam and jibe with fellow artists and poets on verbal and multimedia collaborations.

Tom Sheehan's latest books are *Brief Cases, Short Spans*, and *From the Quickening* (Pocol Press). He has ten Pushcart nominations.

Carolee D. Sherwood is a painter, mixed media artist and poet. She's trained professionally as an expressive arts facilitator and helps others access the healing nature of the arts.

Robert Skiles is an award winning composer, conductor and pianist whose music spans a wide variety of styles and genres; he's recorded and released eight commercially successful CDs of his own music.

Prize-winning photographer **Anne Morrison Smyth** grew up in Ripton, Vermont and in Cambridge, Massachusetts. Anne's love for wildernesses of all kinds informs her work with an intimate, unflinching celebration of the diverse small realities that create a larger truth.

Jessamyn Smyth is a writer in all genres. Her work has been nominated for the Pushcart Prize and recognized in *Best American Short Stories 2006*. She co-edited *qarrtsiluni*'s "Transformation" issue with Allan Peterson.

Luigino Solamito specializes in visual poetry.

Christine Swint is a former high school Spanish teacher who now devotes herself to creative writing and the practice of yoga, and is working on an MFA.

Eileen R. Tabios has released 16 print, four electronic and one CD poetry collections, a novel, an art essay collection, a poetry essay/interview anthology, and a short story book.

Rob Taylor lives in Vancouver, BC by birth and by choice, to greater and lesser degrees of each depending on the weather.

Andrew Topel, standing at 5 feet 11 inches, could indeed be considered short.

Wendy Vardaman has a Ph.D. in English from the University of Pennsylvania. She works for the children's theater company, The Young Shakespeare Players, home schools two of three children, and will soon begin to co-edit the Wisconsin poetry journal *Free Verse*.

Andrea Watson's poetry has appeared in many journals and twice been nominated for the Pushcart Prize. Her traveling show, *Braided Lives: A Collaboration Between Artists and Poets*, was sponsored by the Taos Institute of Arts in July, 2003.

Jill Crammond Wickham is a poet, artist and teacher funding her writing passion by running a children's art studio and gallery. Without collaborative poetry, she would be just another lonely poet, writing in her pajamas.

Scott Wiggerman has published one book of poetry, and been published in dozens of journals. In addition, he is one of the two "cats" (i.e., editors) of *Dos Gatos Press* and editor of the recently published anthology *Big Land, Big Sky, Big Hair*.

Katherine Williams, while making transgenic mice at UCLA, authored three chapbooks, published in various anthologies, and received a Pushcart nomination. She does marine research now and lives with her husband, Richard Garcia (see above) and their dog Louie.

Steve Wing is a visual artist and writer whose work reflects his appreciation for the extraordinary in ordinary days and places. He lives in Florida, where he takes dawn photos on his way to work in an academic institution.

Susan Yount lives on the side of Chicago, works at the Associated Press, pursues her MFA in poetry at Columbia College and is editor and publisher of the *Arsenic Lobster Poetry Journal*.

Joe Zealberg is a psychiatrist in private practice in Charleston, SC. Until now, his publications have been in the field of clinical psychiatry and medicine. He is honored to be Richard Garcia's student, and to be among those called the Long Table Poets.

www.ingramcontent.com/pod-product-compliance
Lightning Source LLC
Chambersburg PA
CBHW070556180626
46817CB00005B/1867